T0354575

Dare and Live

———— ✹ ————

Edgardo G. Calansiñgin

Order this book online at www.trafford.com
or email orders@trafford.com

Most Trafford titles are also available at major online book retailers.

Print information available on the last page.

ISBN: 978-1-4120-5744-8 (sc)
ISBN: 978-1-4122-0036-3 (hc)
ISBN: 978-1-4122-3582-2 (e)

Trafford rev. 06/25/2020

 www.trafford.com
North America & international
toll-free: 1 888 232 4444 (USA & Canada)
fax: 812 355 4082

PROLOGUE

You, too, can dare and still live because you are braver than what you think.

Several war correspondents sought M/Sgt. Jorge G. Herrera, Jr., after World War II ended, for an exclusive interview on his war exploits, but Herrera declined for he felt that the publication of his feat would not accrue to his benefit. It was years later that Jorge G. Herrera, Jr. related to me his role in World War II and it took years before the publication of this book because of publishing financial constraints.

I was skeptical initially of Jorge G. Herrera, Jr.'s account, but I heard some of his exploits during World War II. I was nine years old when I met Jorge G. Herrera, Jr., a year before World War II erupted when he visited his uncle, Teodorico Garagara my maternal grandfather, in his residence at the Bago Ferry Mambucal Bridge. My mother related to me how the Guerrilla Soldiers treated her when she crossed Bago River into the Guerrilla territory; she was detained and questioned for weeks before she was granted an audience with Jorge G. Herrera, Jr., notwithstanding her identity as the first cousin of the Guerrilla Leader. Jorge G. Herrera, Jr. explained to her first cousin that in time of War, he suspected everybody of spying for the Japanese Army, who was out for his capture.

I still had reservation of Jorge G. Herrera, Jr.'s story until the Negros Islands Resistance Movement held its Ruby Anniversary Celebration in 1982 when Veterans of the Negros Islands Resistance Movement held a breakfast meeting with Honorable Ramon Nolan who was an Army Officer and a Member of the Military Court Martial Tribunal in Negros Islands during World War II, and in 1982 President Ferdinand E. Marcos, President of the Philippines appointed Ramon Nolan as the Philippines Ambassador to the United States of America.

Jorge G. Herrera, Jr. brought me along with him into the breakfast meeting in Roli's Refreshment at San Juan Street, Bacolod City. Ramon Nolan rose from his seat from among the many Veterans who were sitting by his side, and approached Jorge G. Herrera, Jr. who was emasculated and a mere shadow of himself by that time when Jorge G. Herrera, Jr. and I entered the Refreshment parlor, and Honorable Ramon Nolan bear-hugged Jorge G. Herrera, Jr.

"Jorge," Honorable Ramon Nolan exclaimed, "We (Members of the Military Court Martial Tribunal) could have sentenced you to a maximum penalty based on the accusations, but we imposed merely a four-month imprisonment because of your excellent war records. Your war achievements might have been duplicated but they could have never been excelled by any other Soldier."

It was this compliment coming from a respected Dignitary that encouraged me into writing this book, not to glorify Jorge G. Herrera, Jr., but illustrate that there was a courageous individual who dared the Japanese Army, fought them against overwhelming odds, and lived to tell his story. Jorge G. Herrera, Jr. penetrated the Japanese Army defense lines, cavorted with the Japanese Soldiers, ambushed and killed thousands of Japanese Soldiers. It might have been due to luck or an act of Providence that M/Sgt. Jorge G. Herrera, Jr. was spared of death, and it seemed that the Japanese Army failed to manufacture the very bullet that would fell the body of Jorge G. Herrera, Jr.

Jorge G. Herrera, Jr. was unschooled (he never completed his elementary education), and he could have never foreseen the value of heroics, but he fought the Japanese Army in Negros Islands like he could repulse the Japanese Forces that landed in Negros Islands and defeated the United States Armed Forces in the Far East. It was during the Ruby Anniversary Celebration of Negros Islands Resistance Movement that the book titled *They Chose To Fight* was published and the book contained the names of the Soldiers who fought against the Japanese Army in Negros Islands during World War II, but one name was missing – Jorge G. Herrera, Jr. I inquired from Jorge G. Herrera, Jr. the reason for the omission of his name from the roster, and he explained that Major Uldarico Baclagon, the author of the book and the Officer whose military orders he countermanded during World War II, had axes to grind against him. The story of Jorge G. Herrera, Jr. needed telling and the following was his narration of the events of World War II from his standpoint.

All the names of the characters in this story came from the lips – dying confession – of M/Sgt. Jorge G. Herrera, Jr., and I assumed that they were all fictitious. Any name referring to any person living or dead; therefore, was a mere coincidence.

The Author

DEDICATION

This Book is dedicated to:

The memory of M/Sgt. Jorge G. Herrera, Jr. who served his Country best during World War II.

The Members of the family of M/Sgt. Jorge G. Herrera, Jr., for their family love and devotion.

The memory of Sgt. Pobleo L. Calansiñgin, who fought in the battlefields of Bataan as an Artilleryman, endured the Death March, was imprisoned and died of starvation and illnesses inside the Japanese Army concentration camp in Camp O'Donnell, Dao, Capas, in Tarlac, the capital of the Province of Tarlac, Philippines. Lt. Elizalde P. Rodrigazo, a family neighbor who survived the Death March and escaped from the Japanese Army Concentration Camp, related to Pobleo's parents the circumstances surrounding the death of their son, when Lieutenant Rodrigazo arrived in Murcia, Negros Islands, less than a year after Pobleo L. Calansiñgin's death.

My family for their encouragement and support.

TABLE OF CONTENTS

CHAPTER 1

War Medals

The long years that had rolled away unnoticed nearly effaced from my faltering mind the memory of World War II. That War which polarized nations into Allied and Axis powers that met in deadly combats in every arena of encounter, seemed like a wisp of smoke that vanished into an empty space leaving no trace of destruction after its wake. Time broke the final link that chained me to the past and the events, which took place during my twenty-fifth year kept slipping away from my parched up brain as I approached the twilight years of my life. Yet now and then, mementoes of that War surfaced and haunted me such that the package that the postman handed me proved of no exception.

The mail bore the Sender's name displayed prominently at the top corner side and read: The United States Department of the Army. Correspondence had long been exchanged between the United States Government and I, that I felt that all the issues between us related to World War II, had long been settled; and there was nothing I expected from the mail but trivial matters. I opened the inconsequential mail at one end and slipped out packets the size of mini boxes. Each box yielded pins, shoulder bars, colorful striped ribbons and glossy brasses. On them the bronze star, symbol of high ideal and noble deed struck prominently to a field of colors. The oak leaf enhanced the beauty of the medal; the shoulder bars were embroidered with colors that were lifted out of the American emblem.

Other embellishment to the medals identified the locality of the war theater where the outstanding deed was achieved. The pins, shoulder bars, ribbons and brasses complimented one with another into an array of war medals.

I threw my mind into frenzy as I wracked up my brain piecing together every bit of the accounts of the events that prompted the United States of America into awarding me the medals, but the passage of time obscured them from recollection. Reminiscing on the best of my war efforts that peaked in a year and a half, the awards granted me averaged a medal for every month of war service. I dwelt lengthily on the evolution of the medals, which proved intriguing, as it was difficult deserving them.

The medals had their origin at the unexplored foothills of the obscure Visayan Islands, some twelve thousand statute miles from Washington D.C. They were mined from streets, farms and mountains of Negros Islands of the Philippines. They were panned from the blood of my countrymen and assayed from the heart of those who selflessly gave up their lives. Numerous death, suffering and heroism eluded the chronicles and they hastily faded into nothingness. The medals solidified the yearnings of the Filipinos for liberty and stoked their quest for freedom and steeled their resolve into a fierce defense of their homeland. They stood for valor and fortitude of the Filipinos in the face of overwhelming odds. The medals were the synthesis of our resistance, adventure and deliverance from the Japanese Army. They were testimony to our close brush with Death.

The Japanese Imperial Forces invasion of the Philippine Islands threw into disarray the war record-keeping system of the United States Armed Forces in the Far East when American and Filipino defenders succumbed to the Japanese Armed Forces superior might. Perimeters were breached, fortifications crumbled, morale shattered and resistance crushed. American and Filipino soldiers perished; some capitulated, others disintegrated into a disorganized retreat. The Filipino Guerrilla Soldiers picked up what were left of the fragmented defense lines and threaded them back into a resistance movement. How the war accounts that took place in the nooks and corners of the more than seven thousands one hundred islands and islets of the Philippine Archipelago, under the most chaotic conditions obtaining in a far-flung, war-torn Far Eastern country, ever reached the war files of the United States Department of the Army in Washington D.C., would always remain a mystery to me.

At an outset, military resistance lay frustrated on the Philippine soil. For some time, a notion of coordinated combat, a muster of combatants, supply of food and arms, vanished into thin air. The vision of nationalism, boldness and freedom flaunted fleetingly in the heart and mind of the Filipinos; but a dream of resistance flashed in the mind of one man, then on another and so on until it conceptualized into a body of fighters capable of challenging the Japanese Imperial Forces. The group snowballed into Guerrilla Fighters that attracted notice of the United States Government. Only then did the Armed Forces of the Philippines revert back to the United States Army.

Once the war reports reached the United States Department of the Army, they were collated and documented. To make sure that the war records remained unaltered, the repository of the annals in the archive was amply secured for posterity. Notwithstanding the gradual metamorphosis of the medals, the United States Government discriminated against wearers of the medals without authority from the Judge Advocate General Office. Aware that the United States of America, proud of her ideals and jealous of her heritage, conferred medals only to the most deserving of the recipients, it dawned on me that in my hands lay a precious trove of commendations.

Today decades after World War II ended, I still derived pleasure in recounting the awards.

United States Government Citations

One – Two Bronze Oak Leaf Cluster Distinguished Unit Emblem
One – Three Bronze Star Asiatic-Pacific Theater Campaign Medal
    with Ribbons

One – World War II Victory Medal
One – Philippine Defense Ribbon with One Bronze Star
One – Philippine Liberation Ribbon with Two Bronze Stars
One – Bronze Star Medal
One – Soldier's Medal
One – Infantry Combat Medal
One – American Service Defense Medal
One – Philippine Independence Medal

Philippine Government Citations

One – Philippine Defense Medal with Ribbons
One – Philippine Liberation Medal with Ribbons
One – Philippine Independence Medal with Ribbons
One – World War II Victory Medal with Ribbons
One – Philippine Republic Presidential Medal Citation Badge
One – American Defense Medal with Ribbons
One – Asiatic-Pacific Theater Medal with Ribbons
One – Distinguished Unit Badge with Oak Leaf Cluster Medal

As I fondled them, flashes of war memories flooded my reveries.

The medals revolved around the enemies, the Japanese Invasion Forces, who played the opposing role in a war script that produced awards. The drama began when the Japanese Forces landed in Bacolod City at the dawn of May 22, 1942, after the bombing of Pearl Harbor in Hawaii, the island hopping in the Far East, the fall of Bataan and Corrigedor Island of the Philippines. The moment the Japanese Forces landed in Negros Islands, Bacolod City seethed in turmoil.

Month's earlier, hectic war preparations were undertaken. Rooftops of buildings were painted black in concealment from reconnoitering enemy planes. Structures were camouflaged with palm tree leaves lending out semblance of a jungle forests when viewed from the air. Nighttime blackouts were strictly imposed in an evasion from detection of a convergent population.

A farmhand underscored the seriousness of the situation when he scaled a coconut tree with flashlight in hand for illumination at nighttime. Hardly had he climbed down the tree when Civilian Volunteer Guards pounced on him, and accusing him of sending coded messages to the Japanese Landing Forces, imprisoned him for espionage.

Able-bodied men, who missed enlistment to the United States Armed Forces in the Far East (USAFFE), were mustered into Home Defense Forces and were designated as Civilian Volunteer Guards, a para-military force. The members of the Civilian Volunteer Guards were sworn in the defense of infrastructures from enemy sabotage and the Watchmen were farmed out to public utilities, depots, vital warehouses, and bridges throughout Negros Islands. For armaments, Teofilo, the local blacksmith took over the challenge. He stoked the embers and the bellows pumped more air into coal of fire. Sheaves of motor vehicle primary and secondary springs were heated red-hot and lay on the anvils; and the hammerings transformed the junks into lethal swords. A *talibong*[1] was two feet long, and two inches wide with pointed tip. The topside was straightened except for a two-inch indentation, which blended with the curving blade to a point. The blade was honed razor-sharp. Hand guard reinforced the hilt, made artistically of carved wood or animal horn, and the saber was sheathed in fanciful scabbard. Slung across the shoulder or secured by a belt around the waist, the talibong was a badge of membership to the Civilian Volunteer Guards militia force. Bago Ferry Mambucal Bridge, a third of a kilometer-long wooden span which linked the Mambucal Cadre to the capital City of Bacolod, merited the services of the Civilian Volunteer Guards because the bridge was the conduit of the logistical line between the remote Mambucal Cadre and the main military installation in Bacolod City. Scores of guards, in shifts, maintained round-the-clock vigil; still the love-struck men among the ranks traversed hills and streams visiting love-sick women in secluded

---

1. Negros Islands native bolo.

hamlets believing that in their humble way, they protected human lives from the onslaught of loneliness and enemy capture.

For ordnance, homemade guns were fashioned out of the motor vehicle steering wheel rod for barrel, and hard wood for stocks. Empty bullet shells of factory-built shotguns were refilled with pointed nails and gunpowder, for bullets. To operate the contraption, the gun barrel was bent at its joint, and the shell was loaded. To reload, the barrel was bent again and the empty shell was pried loose from the gun chamber with the use of a 4-inch nail's head. Another bullet was reloaded and the gun was made ready for firing. Unfortunately, there was insufficient supply of the rods and the scarcity of the gunpowder compounded the situation.

Figure 1 illustrated the inadequacy of arms of the Filipino Civilian Volunteer Guards.

Feeling ran high among the population that the Japanese invaders would land by air. The civilians and the armed militia surmised that by assaulting the airborne Japanese Soldiers while still enmeshed in their parachutes, a killing ratio of ten enemies by a vigilante would repulse the Japanese invasion. Everybody honed their bolos and stocked homemade shotguns and bullets and waited for that fateful day, the moment of the landing of the Japanese Invasion Forces.

When the Japanese warships cut speed towards Banago Wharf in Bacolod City on that misty day of May 22, 1942, a contingent of Filipino soldiers stood guard at the pier ready for the battle against the Japanese Invaders. The artillery guns were zeroed in on the looming Japanese transports and the impatient Filipino soldiers gritted their teeth anxiously waiting for orders into un-leashing the volleys of fire, in hostile reception to the unwelcome foes. The Japanese warships hardly came to full stop when a pall of gloom descended on the ranks of the valiant defenders; the joint United States and the Philippine Military High Commands opted for capitulation, and flashed the order of surrender to all Forces in Negros Islands. The Filipino Soldiers had not yet fully realized the extent of devastations that the Japanese Forces had inflicted on the Filipino and American defenses in Bataan and Corrigedor in Luzon Island. The Japanese Forces had overtaken the Bataan Defenders, killed them or captured them into sub-mission and imprisoned them; while the Defenses in the island of Corrigedor had crumbled. The Japanese Forces wanted the surrender of Negros Islands without a fight and the Defenders saw the futility of resistance. Seeing the white flag, a young Major Ernesto Mata, the Battalion Commander, yanked away the hal-yard and tore the flag of surrender to pieces. Nevertheless, the message of non-resistance must be conveyed from post to post, and a delegation of soldiers was dispatched to the Mambucal Cadre in the dissemination of the unfortunate news along the route, until the Delegation met another Convoy from Mambucal Cadre who was enroute to Bacolod City. Apprised of the disheart-ening edict, the Junior Officer in charge of the Convoy grabbed the flag of truce that was moored to the Delegation's vehicle, tore it and tossed the flag of surrender away while tears streamed down his faces. The spirits of the young Battalion Commander and the Junior Officer epitomized the Negros Islands' resistance to the Japanese Forces invasion of Negros Islands.

Figure 2 depicted Japanese Warships landing in Bacolod City on May 22, 1942.

People who had inkling of the enemy landing that fateful dawn deserted the City. Owners of vast tracts of land who resided in the metropolis headed to their farms. Residents forsook estates and homes and dispersed to the countryside. Businessmen closed shops and abandoned their establishments. Men and women; young or old fled from the approaching Japanese Invading Forces. Everyone carried on one's person what one deemed the most essential item for use in a day-to-day struggle for survival while away from home. The poor who had no earthly possessions suddenly found windfalls among the foodstuffs, goods and clothing lying around and abandoned by the people who scampered hurriedly, fearful of the arrival of the Japanese Soldiers. The destitute had their fill in the picking when other people deposited their loots a distance away while coming back for more and found to their chagrin that other poor souls had scooped away their unguarded booty while they turned their back. Trucks, automobiles, carts, sleds, and other means of improvised transports teeming with people's earthly possessions, trekked out of the capital city. People who loaded themselves with whatever they could possibly accommodate on pates, backs, shoulders and arms, fled without hope of ever coming back home. Those who were indifferent, skeptical, and lazy or those who were caught unaware were in for big surprises of their lives. When they woke up early morning of May 22, 1942, they mistook for City Policemen the khaki uniformed Japanese Army Soldiers directing City traffics for the Japanese Imperial Forces had landed!

The Japanese slanting eye corners and thick eyebrows with oval faces set them apart from the Filipinos. They were in full battle regalia; tan helmet and brown, short-sleeved shirts. At Garrison duties, they wore elongated, visor caps with sun guard flapping down their nape. Across their shirt, leather straps slung over their shoulders holding up the back of their pants to the front of their trousers.

Figure 3 portrayed a fully armed Japanese Soldier.

Sheathed bayonet and the ubiquitous water canteen and packets of bullets hanged from a belt wrapped around their waist. They wore baggy pants but woolen straps bandaged them around their legs. Standing five feet five inches on the average on bow-arched legs and canvas shoes, they walked slightly astride with rifle slung over their shoulder. The Officers, on the other hand, wore visor caps without sun guard but they sported sidearm and a samurai sword. A Japanese soldier appeared meek and gentle so many Filipinos failed rendering him homage – bowing one's head to the level of one's waist.

Trouble then began!

Sensing trouble from the Japanese soldiers, Filipino comrades were driven to their wit's end drawing up plans of alliances for survival, and on many occasions, agreements were conveniently put aside in promotion of selfish interests and for personal survival; such as the plan agreed upon between the Murcia Town Police Force and the remnants of the USAFFE Soldiers who refused the surrender. The Municipal Police Force in Murcia was under the supervision of the Town Mayor who was answerable to the Provincial Governor who held office in Bacolod City. When the Japanese Army landed, indecision plagued government official-dom; since there was no clear-cut government policy of dealing locally with the Japanese Army, from the National Government in Manila. The Murcia Town Police Force was in quandary between abandonment of the Post with the weapons or submission to the Japanese Army. The Japanese Army was expected momentarily in the town that would demand complete accountability of weapons in the Municipal Town Police Force arsenal. The group of the non-surrendered USAFFE Soldiers, on the other hand, demanded the turnover of the weapons with veiled threats of branding the Policemen traitors and their refusal of non-cooperation, a serious offense that merited death. The Town Police Force and the USAFFE Soldiers contrived a plan of alibi before the Japanese Army with the USAFFE Soldiers staging a nighttime raid of the Municipality for the confiscation of the weaponry, and the Town Policemen cooperating and handing all the armaments to the raiding party.

The USAFFE Soldiers emerged from darkness at the appointed time of the night, and the Town Policemen welcomed their compatriots with open arms, but the atmosphere tensed abruptly and the night reeked with hostilities. The Raiders rounded up all the unsuspecting Town Policemen, maltreated them, hogtied the Policemen like animals destined to slaughterhouses, and dumped them into ditches. Demands for explanation drew the Commandeers' wrath. The Hosts were pummeled and butted with rifles while the Raiders hauled away the arsenal's contents, leaving the Policemen lying helplessly on the ground. When the Policemen freed themselves, they dashed to freedom and headed to the mountains before the Japanese Army exacted retributions.

The Japanese Army wasted no time in spreading into all directions. They took control of the Mambucal Cadre and set up a contingent of their soldiers under the command of Lieutenant Sakai. In an afternoon, Lieutenant Sakai and three of his soldiers commuted to Bacolod City from the Mambucal Cadre. Lieutenant Sakai's driver noticed a log lay across the road, eight kilometers from the Mambucal Cadre. The Japanese soldiers disembarked and cleared the road, when volleys of fire ensued. The Japanese Soldier fired back, but they were no matches to the Ambushers who were well concealed and in a better attacking position than the Japanese Convoy. The Ambushers killed the Japanese soldiers except for Lieutenant Sakai who was left for dead. When Lieutenant Sakai regained consciousness, he stripped off his military uniforms, and set foot three kilometers northwest of the ambush site to *Hacienda Paz*[2], located a couple of kilometers west of Bago Ferry Mambucal Bridge that intercepted the highway six kilometers east to Mambucal Cadre and eight kilometers west to the Municipality of Murcia. How Lieutenant Sakai succeeded in passing himself off as a native Filipino, along

---

2. Sugarcane plantation owned by Paz family.

the route, piqued me; and why he picked Hacienda Paz among the many places around the ambush site, intrigued me more. The moment the wounded Japanese Officer reached Hacienda Paz, the laborers of the plantation, loaded Lieutenant Sakai on a cargo truck and transported him back to the Mambucal Cadre where he was provided with first aid medical treatment. The Japanese Lieutenant was bandaged heavily from head to foot and he was rushed to Bacolod City to the Japanese Army General Headquarters hospital for medical treatment.

The Japanese Imperial Army tightened its grips of Bacolod City and Negros Islands. They occupied large and vital buildings and posted sentries to the City entrances and exits. Magsuñgay, a creek running from north to west at the southeastern rampart of Bacolod City abetted the Japanese Army defenses. The bridges were guarded but many points along the Creek were left to foot patrols. Bakyas was the least guarded of the points and Filipino Civilians inhabited the tract of land along the creek, some of which spied for the Japanese Army. Many of the traitors were City dwellers who tipped off the Japanese Army of the Guerrilla Soldiers' presence in the vicinity, because the tip-offs became lucrative sources of income for them. A scalawag went to the extent of dropping surreptitiously slugs into the pockets of a rough neck, and tipped off the Japanese Army. The Japanese Soldiers arrested the innocent, dragged him away and executed him to death for a measly sum of money.

With Cesar Sarito, Cenon Gatuslao, Elpidio Macasa, Jose Lo, Jose Diaz and others, I departed for Bacolod City. I had stashed arm caches around the discarded USAFFE Depot and I wanted them recovered. At Bakyas, the spies challenged our entry, but many of them were my City acquaintances so I proposed that they let us in unmolested or we blast our way in. To drive home our point, my men and I bared our torsos and disclosed the grenades hidden under our shirts. Unfastening a couple of the grenades, I pulled off the safety pins and dare the spies got their worst. The traitors balked at the idea, because they realized the vulnerability of their families to our retaliation and the weaklings cleared our way and they spared us of Japanese Army detection. We went to the Depot, dug out the arms, loaded them on *caretellas*[3] and rode through a fast exit. I ventured alone inside the City, on several occasions later on, walking as if there was no war at all, and I was fortunate that I did not encounter a Japanese Spy or a Japanese Soldier.

Pedro Alit was not as lucky as I was. His rival for a lady's hand turned into an enemy hack. Pedro had secretly joined an underground movement against the Japanese Army before he slipped inside the City when Juanito Diaz, Pedro's rival, spotted him, and accosted Pedro who had no chance of escape. With tinge of vengeance seething down deep in his heart, Juanito wanted Pedro Alit dragged to the nearest Japanese Sentry. Manuel Salazar, a mutual friend, entreated Juanito Diaz from endorsing Pedro Alit to the Japanese Army and proposed that for friendship's sake, he (Manuel) should likewise be handed over together with Pedro Alit to the Japanese Army, should Juanito insisted on betraying a mutual friend. Juanito relented in acquiesce to the entreaty of Manuel Salazar; Pedro Alit was spared of arrest by the Japanese Army; and if not for the intercession of Manuel Salazar, the Japanese Army could have executed Pedro Alit and Juanito Diaz could have exacted his revenge.

Pedro Alit's daring penetration of the Japanese Army encirclement persisted until next time when his luck ran out; Juanito finally obtained his retribution and delivered him to the Japanese Army. The Japanese Soldiers arrested Pedro Alit, imprisoned him and subjected him to incessant interrogations. The Japanese Army wanted the admission of his membership to the Guerrilla Movement and the Japanese Soldiers wanted concrete information on the memberships and whereabouts of the clandestine organization. Pedro Alit's denials infuriated the Japanese Army Interrogators and the Japanese Guards rained blows of rough lumber slabs on his frail body. The blows caused contusions, wilted skin, bloodied body and head; still Pedro Alit stood pat on his

---

3. Horse drawn two-wheeled, two-passenger couch.

denials. The Japanese Army sentenced Pedro Alit to death and asked for his last wishes. Pedro Alit figured out his dilemma. If he should choose life over death, he would betray his companions and the number of fatalities would increase because many of comrades were married and had families. He resigned to death, his fate and enjoined the Japanese Army the remittance of his cadaver to the care of his parents. Pedro Alit entreated the Japanese Army Executioners into granting him a moment of prayer before his life was snuffed out. The Japanese Soldiers, hearing Pedro Alit's plea, had a change of heart and concluded that Pedro Alit was an innocent man. The Japanese Army set him free!

The Japanese Army wasted no time in the extension of their sphere of influence from Bacolod City, east to the Municipality of Murcia and subjected the town to sporadic incursions. It was not unusual for town residents being aroused by staccato of gun fires at the earliest dawn when sleep was at its deepest point. A resident who fled towards the luxuriant sugarcane fields was rained with bullets and massacred before he made good his escape. The unpredictable raids of the Japanese Army in Murcia drove the Filipino Civilians away from the town, so the Japanese Army encouraged the population back to the town. Murcia was festive at times and people seemed oblivious to the onset of war, especially on market days when the populace from neighboring *barrios*[4] converged in the *poblacion*[5] on Sundays, the town's market day. The town had a quadrangle surrounded by shop, store, saloon, cafeteria and market booths. The structures served as convergence places for transient travelers, merchants, strangers, relatives, friends and spies. The quadrangle was where the Japanese Puppet Philippine President Jose P. Laurel delivered speeches in behalf of the Japanese Government, urging the Filipino people cooperation with the Japanese Government after the Japanese Army rounded, on a Sunday, the town people for compulsory attendance to the meeting. Without newspaper publication and

---

4. Philippine smallest political subdivision.
5.. Town square.

radio broadcasting, news reports circulated by whispers, rumors and innuendoes with updates passed on to the next person by word of mouth.

Words reached Felipe Lumacang while he was inside a cafeteria that a Japanese Patrol arrived in town. From past experiences, the Filipinos learned bitter lesson that it was an imprudent stratagem fleeing from the presence of the Japanese Soldiers for the Japanese Soldiers shot at anybody who fled from their presence, believing that a fleer was a remnant of the USAFFE Soldiers. Felipe Lumacang calculated that by the time he received the news report, the town had probably been cordoned with concealed Japanese Sentries while group of Japanese Soldiers combed the marketplace, hunting down and rounding up males of major age whom they gathered beside the town square. Felipe was one of the captives who were lined up before a sack-hooded, but authoritative man whose white eyeballs were discernable but the remaining features of his body were hidden from view, and the Japanese Army Spy remained unidentified. Each captive stepped forward before the shrouded man and those he indicated to with a nod of his head were segregated to one side where the watchful Japanese Soldiers stood guard around them. Felipe Lumacang was one of those pointed at by the cloaked Japanese Army Spy and ropes, precluding any chance of his escape, bound him. The captives were spared of imprisonment in the town Municipal Building; instead they were loaded into a crammed van and hauled to Bacolod City.

Felipe was confined inside a cell of the Provincial High School building in Bacolod City; he was tied to a post inside the prison cell and he abandoned completely any thought of escape. The Japanese Army interrogations became a daily routine and his denials of the Japanese Army Interrogators' accusations of his involvement with the Resistance Movement against the Japanese Army, infuriated the Japanese Soldiers. The Japanese Guards took turns in beating him with pieces of woods and they never cared where the truncheons landed so his body wilted. The Japanese Soldiers inquisitions went on and punishments were inflicted everyday against his frail body causing pain over the area of his lungs; Felipe's breathing shortened with every inhalation becoming a struggle for thin air, but the Japanese Soldiers never relented on their brutality until their ferociousness was satiated. Felipe Lumacang's steadfast protestations of his innocence paid off when his sisters pleaded, day by day, to the Japanese Army for clemency and the Japanese Army released him from incarceration after weeks of cruelty. Felipe Lumacang, once acquitted and released from captivity by the Japanese Army headed straight to my hideout and enlisted with my Guerrilla Band, and together, we fought against the Japanese Forces until World War II ended.

The Japanese Army never spared farmland regions like Hacienda Makilan, which was located six kilometers southeast of the town of Murcia. Hacienda Makilan was bordered with bamboo trees and the Japanese Patrol approaches to the region were hidden from view of the village populace. Enrique Ariñas, a former Murcia town policeman who figured earlier in the guerrilla arms raid of the town, joined a different band of guerrilla soldiers and became its food procurement member. He was in Hacienda Makilan where he was busy loading sacks of palay into *carabao*[6] sleds for transport to the mountain hideouts and oblivious of the approaching Japanese Patrol when the Japanese Soldiers; their helmets were camouflaged with grasses, materialized among the surrounding greeneries and caught Enrique Ariñas in total surprise. Enrique Ariñas pretended himself as one of the villagers when he realized that escape was impossible. The Japanese Soldiers arrested him, and never questioned him; instead the Japanese Soldiers probed his palms, forefingers, and shoulders. Fortunately, Enrique Ariñas was a non-combatant member of the guerrilla band and he had not handled, carried or fired a rifle; nevertheless, the Japanese Army suspected him as a guerrilla soldier, bound his hands behind his back, and marched him ahead of the Japanese Patrol column. He sensed a gnawing fear building from within for he had a feeling that somewhere along the

---

6. Water buffalo.

line, the Japanese Soldiers would shot him to death. The Japanese Patrol had distanced a couple of kilometers away when the Japanese Soldiers shouted frantically to Enrique, ordering him to lay down flat to the ground while the Japanese Soldiers spread and fired at their targets, leaving Enrique Ariñas momentarily unguarded and hidden behind an anthill. Enrique Ariñas saw the opportunity he was silently praying for; so he lunged forward, rolled over, and risking the danger of stray bullets, dashed away to freedom. It was concomitant that during the encounter, my Guerrilla Band freed Enrique Ariñas, who belonged to another guerrilla outfit, from the capture of the Japanese Army. When we saw the Japanese Patrol intruding into my sub-command post at *Sitio*[7] Udag, my Guerrilla Soldiers launched an offensive with the purpose of driving away the Japanese Forces from our sources of food supply in the region. We wounded eight Japanese Soldiers during the skirmishes and the Japanese Patrol carted away in sleds their casualties.

The Japanese Army occupied finally the town of Murcia, and constructed an observation post on top of the 50-foot concrete Municipal Building, which stood on a town that was a thousand feet above sea level. The Japanese Soldiers observation tower provided them with unhampered view over the surrounding regions kilometers away from the Municipal Building. Houses and the occupants' daily activities on orchard yards were closely monitored with the use of binoculars. Villages that were concealed from view by cloistered trees and vegetation were bombarded unexpectedly with mortar blasts from the observation tower or the Japanese Foot Patrol swooped down on the unwary inhabitants. The Japanese Army sent out Patrol Soldiers in all directions in accordance with their program of conquests.

Pacifico Salanap avoided opposition to the Japanese Forces and opted for a life of a non-combatant; he constructed an abode on a distant village making his shanty visible to the Japanese Army monitoring system from the town, and he lived the life of a farmer.

---

7. A small and temporary political subdivision.

Pacifico Salanap, like other farmers, realized the dwindling food supply because the farmers spent more time evading the Japanese Soldiers than time spent on food production. He resorted to edibles procured on resources at hand, and one of them was from the abundance of *tibagrings*[8] that infested the *palay*[9] plants. The grasshoppers were mobile at daylight but they perched on palay stalks and the insects were tame at night. Pacifico needed nighttime illumination in gathering the edible grasshoppers, and he discovered that the railroad track combustible wooden ties, which had been treated with asphalt, served his purpose for the nocturnal safari. He set out with a group of his friends to Hacienda San Bernabe, five kilometers from his home, and they dug away the wooden planks from the railroad track. They chose the portion of railway that cut through and lay between banks of earth which was once a hill; the place was a couple of kilometers from the town garrison of the Japanese Army, was hidden from view from the national highway, and no one in the group ever thought of the Japanese Army discovering them. The Sugar Mills stopped milling sugar canes and abandoned the railways when war broke out, but the Japanese Army prohibited their destruction. The Japanese Army decreed that divestment of the railway structures was an act of sabotage and was punishable with death by firing squad. A dozen of men that composed the group were so engrossed in the excavation of the wooden planks that they botched the approach of the Japanese Foot Patrol. The uncanny crackles of the Japanese Soldiers rifles jolted them into stark reality that escape was impossible. The Japanese Patrol lined up the filchers in a row facing the firing squad and the Japanese Soldiers let loose the barrage that raked the victims to the ground. The group, a bloody heap, lay on the ground lifeless; except for Pacifico Salanap who after hearing of the departing footsteps wriggled out at the wrong time because one of the *Japanese (JP) Police*[10] caught glimpse of Pacifico's movement and the Japanese Soldiers

---

8. Edible grasshoppers of locust specie.
9. Unhusked rice grain.
10. Filipinos who enlisted into the Japanese Army.

came back for his execution. The Japanese Soldiers set him up and the firing squad aimed their rifles at him. Pacifico, by some dint of luck, anticipated the volley of fires, fell to the ground as if he was hit, and lay very still among the dead corpses of his fallen companions and feigned death. The Japanese Patrol left Pacifico for dead. Pacifico Salanap survived the Japanese Army execution but he was wounded when the United States Liberation Forces strafed Murcia Municipal Building with aircraft machineguns in the initial phase of the town liberation from the Japanese Army. The United States aircrafts flew over Pacifico's house in their strafing loops; and Pacifico got so enthusiastic of the liberation that he waved white clothing to the aircrafts, his way of expressing elation over the Japanese Army annihilation and his way of thanking the pilots of the United States Air Force; but he stood on a spot designated by the Liberation Forces as war zone; so he became suspect to the attacking United States Air Force warplanes and one of the warplanes came back at him and strafed him. He ran for cover in the ditches, but a bullet found its mark. The strafing from the aircraft machinegun hit him on the stomach leaving an inch-deep grazing wound, and fortunately, the bullet failed the penetration into his internal organs. He got out of the canal and managed his way into his hut nearby. Pacifico's wounds healed after months of ministration with the use of gunpowder in place of medicine and in the absence of proper medical attention and lack of drugs. If there was such a thing as luck, Pacifico Salanap had three; for he cheated death when the Japanese Army executed him twice and he survived the United States Liberation Warplane .50 Caliber Machinegun bullet on his stomach.

The Japanese Patrol almost caught my Guerrilla Band while we were in Barrio Sum-ag, a location six kilometers south of Bacolod City. The National Highway parted the Barrio into eastern and western sections; the eastern zone was densely populated and the place was vegetated with coconut and bamboo trees, while the western sector was less populated, although planted with coconut and bamboo trees, led to the beaches. The Japanese Patrol left their vehicles before the Sum-ag River Bridge, which served as an entranceway into the Barrio and walked on foot; thus, their approaches were unnoticed and my Guerrilla Soldiers were caught off guard. If my group dashed towards the eastern sector and fled towards the direction of the mountains, the Japanese Patrol would block our path and mowed us down with machinegun fires; the civilian population would be caught in a cross-fire, a situation which we avoided desperately. We opted for the maneuver towards the seashore and I posted my Soldiers behind coconut trees; our options were a pretense of being beach bathers should the Japanese Patrol found their way towards us or a fight behind coconut or bamboo trees and out of the jam. Fortunately, the Japanese Soldiers went the other way.

The Japanese Army held vicious sway over Negros Islands for three long years; and they were ferocious Conquerors as they suspected males of membership to the USAFFE and they wedged vise-grip hold on the lives of the Filipino people in the city and towns, and pursued indefatigably the trails of the USAFFE Soldiers and the Filipino Guerrilla Soldiers. The Japanese Patrol roused town people from deep slumber at the unholy hours with staccato of gun fires resulting into indiscriminate deaths of the defenseless and the unfortunate. There were many Japanese Nationals, who had resided for long period of time in the Philippines as trades men and merchants, but when the Japanese Forces landed in the Philippines, the Japanese Nationals became officers of the Japanese Invasion Forces, and others who had knowledge of city and town geography, aided the Japanese Army in search of their Filipino enemies. The Japanese Army had great advantage over the Filipino Civilians and the Guerrilla Soldiers because they possessed vehicles, which they utilized whenever, and wherever they went in search of the suspected Guerrilla Soldiers. The Japanese Army had also the luxury of using their warplanes in the reconnaissance of the suspected lairs of the Guerrilla Soldiers, strafing them with machine guns or dropping bombs on suspected places. The Filipino Civilians and the Guerrilla Soldiers defenses were merely flight on foot. The Japanese Soldiers searched dwellings, waylaid innocent travelers on pathways, and crisscrossed river banks where refugees, in caves and thickets hid, killing the men, violating the women and bayoneting to death even the children.

The succeeding chapters chronicled the ignominy of defeat, the birth of the guerrilla movement, near shoot-out among comrades, the stab of treachery, the romance of a bivouac, the secret of intelligence network, the dragnet of capture, the pangs of starvation, the shadow of hopelessness, the glimmer of hope, the joy of victory, and the glory of freedom. The annals of our travails and triumphs were memories of World War II and our exploits were the alloys that forged the War Medals.

CHAPTER 2

Usaffe

The year was 1937 and the Philippine Commonwealth Government summoned 20-year olds for compulsory military training. The lure of military life beckoned me and I was titillated. Years earlier, my mother died at an age that deprived me of a vivid recollection of her, and my mother's brother, Teodorico Garagara, my uncle related to me how life was hard for me even at my tender age, for the midwife who attended to my birth panicked when she failed at freeing me out of the embryonic sac. She ran for a pair of scissors and incised me out of the thickest embryonic sac she had ever encountered throughout her professional life. Years later, a Palm Reader analyzed my palms and she predicted a very precarious life for me. It appeared that it was impossible for my brother, the only children in the family, of surviving together with me. The Palm Reader predicted that should I live; my brother would perish, and true enough, my brother died. A Soothsayer hazarded further my future; I would become a tamer of wild animals, however, instead of seeking a job as a circus animal handler's handyman, I enrolled in a Military Cadre as a member of the first batch of the Military Trainees in Mambucal Cadre.

The Mambucal Cadre squatted on a government forest reservation at the foot of Mount Canlaon, fourteen kilometers east from Bacolod City, the capital of Negros Occidental province in

Negros Islands. The tract of land was a plateau of stones, boulders, rocks, trees and reeds. Once cleared, the campus was transformed into quadrangles of barracks and training ground. Tall trees and thickets that thrived along the creek, which ran beside the camp, served as buffers to the shooting ranges. The Trainees clad in *maong*[11] pants, shirts, and caps, tanned under the heat of the summer sun on barren, red-clayed ground. We drilled daily in battle formations. We advanced, with bayonets fixed to our rifles, against imaginary enemies, the stuffed scarecrows and banana stalks. We lurched forward. We thrust. We withdrew our rifles, parried, butted and attacked our targets. We spent considerable time in marksmanship practice. We simulated battlefield scenarios and we adopted tactical assaults. We trained on synchronizing the movements of the Infantry Division with the Medical Battalion under hostile conditions. The hectic military exercises were broken only when the Soldiers were marched down the river for swimming exercises. Hiking six kilometers down to Bago River Ferry Mambucal Bridge, we simulated troop movements and battle skirmishes; and we were rewarded with the luxury of an exhilarating frolic of mass bathing in the cool water of Bago River.

The Commonwealth of the Philippine Government suspended the Cadre training program in Mambucal after five and a half months; and I found myself jobless on the streets until two years later when another Summon came. The Call was for the purpose of completing the 11-month compulsory Military Training for every 20-year old Filipino male. I reported to the Binalbagan Cadre under a new set of Officers who proved to be strict disciplinarians. Military Officers like Colonel Eulalio Tañedo, Colonel Benito Valeriano and Lieutenant-Colonel Tiburcio Ballesteros who etched their names in the rosters of the Philippine Army Hall of Fame, played important roles in shaping my military life. The Training proved more advanced than previously; and upon completion of the Course in December 1940, another interruption to the Training Program occurred.

---

11. Cotton cloth dyed in blue-black color.

I enlisted into the Commonwealth of the Philippine Regular Army and I was assigned to the 2nd Quartermaster Company, General Depot in Binalbagan, Negros Occidental. I was privileged of attending the General Military Troop School in Luzon Island, during the year, where I assimilated lessons that proved later very valuable in my combat encounters. When I completed the General Military Troop School course on December 8, 1941, I reported immediately to Headquarters 7th Military District and Headquarters District Quartermaster General Depot in Camp Araneta, Binalbagan, Negros Occidental under the command of an American Officer, Colonel Hillsman who was succeeded later on by Major Crisanto P. Vidamo as my Commanding Officer and Lieutenant Nakar as his Adjutant.

Contrary to the military discipline that I imbibed I came into grips with my officers and fellow soldiers. My carefree, devilish and mischievous ways got into their nerves; in exasperation, Major Vidamo summoned me to his Office, and he demanded to know whether I wanted to be in or out of the Army. I had experimented taking on varied odd jobs in the past without success for I disliked the drudgery of errands where I felt like a square peg in a round hole when it came to civilian tasks. There was no other way left for me but stick to the Army and Major Vidamo assented to my choice, while he lectured me with stern admonitions:

"Herrera," Major Vidamo's voice boomed with paternal tones. "If you wanted to stay in the Army, stay with me!"

"If you wanted to be a good soldier, stay with me!" he exhorted.

"And if you wanted to be an Officer, stay with me!" Major Vidamo urged me in a voice that rang with finality.

My performances improved to the delight of the good Major. It was of common knowledge that many of my fellow soldiers envied me when I started earning chevrons as badges of promotion for what took my contemporaries probably years of endeavor before earning them, I collected the stripes in six months; and on top of it all, I was a Sergeant in charge of the procurement of all military supplies for the 7th Military District. My assignments were errand chores for the Army, but I relished the daily trip north 82 kilometers to Bacolod City in a chauffeured-driven car, and side trips for a visit to girlfriends. I canvassed prices of military supplies sold in stores in Bacolod City, and I submitted the quotations to the Quartermaster before the military supplies were purchased for the 7th Military District. I recommended the lowest prices of the military supplies as well as suggested the best Suppliers of the goods, and my recommendations were always approved to the letter.

Military Officers like Major Vidamo, Lieutenant +Nakar and others, were paragons of virtue because the Philippine Army dealt severe punishment otherwise; but to claim that we detested "*extras*"[12] would be an understatement. Big Suppliers of military materials in Bacolod City, in an effort of ingratiating themselves with me and cornering the business patronage of the 7th Military District, packed my car with *extras* against my vehement protests; because the stiff competition among the Suppliers forced them into outbidding each other.

A Soldier had a monthly clothing allowance, which the Philippine Army provided consistently; but I saved on my monthly clothing allowances and I still had ample supply of khaki uniforms because Suppliers stuffed my car with extra khaki clothing materials. Patrons of considerable means gifted me with expensive suiting materials and expensive shoes; that had I have an opportunity of displaying my civilian clothes, I could have been mistaken for a rich sugar baron with impeccable taste for clothing made of the *de Hilo*[13] suits and Florisheim shoes; but since I had no relatives around me, the extra goods ended up as gifts to my friends.

Major Vidamo would have appeared naked without a cigar stuffed halfway into his mouth, for he was a chain-smoker. Lieutenant Nakar loved the best of the wine, for he was a wine connoisseur and my driver would never settle for locally manufactured cigarettes for we all loved imported goods; so I kept the

---

12. Tips tendered voluntarily.
13. First class suiting material made of cotton.

cigar boxes filled, the best kind of wine in stock, and imported cigarettes in affluence. To satisfy the curiosity of other officers and fellow soldiers on the sources of our endless supply, I offered those lame excuses, a knowing smile and a wink of an eye. When Major Vidamo got wind of an Order transferring me to the Mambucal Cadre, he lost no time in countermanding the reassignment to the full acquiescence of Lieutenant Nakar, for I became their *niño bonito*[14].

On December 23, 1941, the Philippine Army of the Commonwealth Government of the Philippine Islands was inducted into the United States Armed Forces in the Far East (USAFFE). When World War II broke out in December 1941, military training and troop movements were intensified. News of World War II coming to the Philippine shores caused transport of several Army Divisions of Filipino Soldiers coming from the Military Cadres of the different towns in Negros Islands. The Philippine Government commandeered public transportations operating in Negros Islands and utilized them for troop movements. Buses were painted tan brown, the Army color and were converted into military vehicles. Fifty or more of the trucks were lined up in single file column and the vehicles traveled a unit away from each other and shuttled back and forth, night and day, between the military cadres and the disembarkation points in Pulupandan or Banago Ports. They were filled with soldiers; as they shuttled back and forth with dimmed headlights to the soldiers' disembarkation points at the wharves. Hundreds of truckloads of Filipino Soldiers from Mambucal Cadre 34 kilometers east of Bacolod City, Fabrica Cadre 80 kilometers north of Bacolod City, Magallon Cadre 90 kilometers southeast of the City, Kabankalan Cadre 100 kilometers and Binalbagan Cadre 85 kilometers south of Bacolod City; all boarded ships at Pulupandan and Banago Ports. Our Regiment was left behind for lack of sea transport. For lack of transportation, a Medical Battalion from Mambucal Cadre hiked the 34-kilometer distance to Banago Pier in catch-

---

14. Favorite soldier.

ing up with the sea transport. Thousands of the Filipino Soldiers boarded the military ships and landed ultimately in Bataan and Corrigedor Island; but very few ever came back.

When news reports of the Philippine and American Military defeats in Luzon Island seeped down to Negros Islands, the public became apprehensive of troop movements and they equated military maneuvers with the invasion of Negros Islands; so we moved in martial simulation halfway to Bacolod City and stayed temporarily in the town of La Carlota where we occupied the school grounds and school buildings. It was on December 20, 1941 when Colonel Hillsman, Major Vidamo and other Officers laid out plans for troop dispersal, which was implemented immediately. On January 2, 1942, Headquarters District Quartermaster, General Depot of the 7th Military District Headquarters under Lieutenant-Colonel Richard I. Jones as Depot Commander and Major Crisanto P. Vidamo as his Deputy Commander, moved to Bacolod City.

The USAFFE General Depot occupied half of a City block; bounded by Lacson Street in the west, Rizal Street in the north, Gonzaga Street in the south, and Mabini Street in the east. A two-storey building occupied two and a half hectares of the block; and the massive concrete building was laden with military supplies to the brim that I felt the contents would last longer than I expected. I was the Supply Sergeant of the Depot and my job consisted of loading the warehouse and distributing the supplies to which ever Military Commander in Negros Islands that requisitioned for logistics. I commandeered, in name of the United States Armed Forces in the Far East, items I deemed necessary for the use of the Military. I meandered in Negros Islands and claimed for the USAFFE items such as weapons, ammunitions, vehicles, sugar, rice, corn, salt, kerosene, alcohol, and medicine. Household items such as needles, threads, china wares and matches became part of the stock supply from the Donors who were individuals, commercial establishments, companies, single proprietors, and corporations. I received officially whatever supplies placed under my custody from *SS PANAY*, the

supply ship transporting military supplies from Luzon Island to
Negros Islands.

The last voyage of SS PANAY ended in a disaster when the Japanese Navy torpedoed the supply vessel and inflicted on it irreparable damage; instead of docking at Pulupandan Wharf, its usual port of call, SS PANAY altered its course and sank in Maricalum, a temporary docking point in southeastern Negros Islands. On February 10, 1942, I led a Security Detail that convoyed the shipment of rifles, pistols, and rounds of ammunitions that were salvaged from the ill-fated SS PANAY and I deposited the arsenals in my Depot. The USAFFE General Depot contained 155mm Cannons, 105mms, Enfields, Garands, .45 Cal. Pistols, Grenades, and boxes containing millions of rounds of ammunitions. The warehouse was filled to the rafter with arms, ammunitions, food, clothing, medicines, and household supplies.

Most of the supplies were transported later to Masulog when it became apparent that the Japanese Army was landing in Negros Islands. Masulog was a mountain fortress with rugged terrains for difficult access and caves for storage spaces. Masulog was considered the best Supply Depot for a retreating USAFFE Army defending Negros Islands from the mountains, against the superior Japanese Army attacking from the Negros Islands coastlines. Day and night, truckloads of supplies were rushed to the secret mountain warehouses while at the same time, requisitions of the different Army Commanders were filled up and their reserved stocks were beefed up; but time was running out. The Japanese Forces got impatient with the outcome of fruitless negotiations for surrender with the USAFFE Command; and the Japanese Army served notice of the invasion of Negros Islands, with or without the surrender of the USAFFE Army. The Japanese Army invasion of Negros Islands; therefore, became imminent with timing as the only remaining question. As days passed, the continued transport of military supplies from the USAFFE Depot in Bacolod City to the mountain fortress became an exercise in futility. With few remaining days before the Japanese Forces landed in Bacolod City, I was left with a discretion of disposing of the remaining military supplies in the USAFFE Depot in Bacolod City; and I was weighed down with indecision as I agonized over the idea of keeping the supplies intact for the United States Armed Forces in the Far East (USAFFE) and the onus of denying the Japanese Forces of war materials left inside the Depot.

I decided that I disposed off all the contents of the USAFFE Depot before the war materials fell into the hands of the Japanese Invading Forces; so I devised a scheme. I spirited a truckload of weapons and ammunitions to Barrio Cansilayan 22 kilometers southeast of Bacolod City, and hid the arm cache inside a cave that was once a part of a Sugar Mill during the Spanish Era, at the bank of Bago River. Members of the families of Claridad, Guzon, and Banay and many others trusted relatives and friends stood guard over the arsenal. Back to Bacolod City, I buried hand grenades, automatic pistols, and rounds of ammunitions around the base of the walls of the USAFFE Depot; and I marked the spots for easy recovery of my stash.

My stint with the USAFFE Depot and my stay around the warehouse enabled me into establishing rapports among the residents in the area. It was ironic that the security-conscious United States Army chose Gonzaga Street for the site of the USAFFE Depot because right at the back of the Warehouse were residences of the Japanese Nationals like the families of Ishwata, Takahasi, Nakano, Masunaga, Togue, Watanabe, and Tanaka who were old-time residents of Bacolod City and had their houses built around the Military Supply Depot. The Japanese Nationals were all locked up behind the USAFFE stockades; except for the children of Katchumbo Togue and Hakaro Tanaka. I was smitten with love to Mereza Tanaka, daughter of Hakaro Tanaka, a Japanese National and a Filipino; and with the help of prominent residents I was permitted by the USAFFE into vouching for the loyalty of Mereza's family, the Tanaka children and the children of Togue who were the Tanaka's family friend. The Tanaka and the Togue children aided me into spreading out the news to all others in the area into helping themselves to all the supplies left inside the Depot before the remainder were set to flames lest the supplies fell into the Japanese Army hands. With people scurrying like pismires from all directions the Warehouse was emptied of its contents before the Japanese Forces landed in Negros Islands, and Bacolod City fell at the dawn of May 22, 1942.

With the USAFFE Military Command dispersed in Bacolod City, I went into hiding with Mereza Tanaka's family in Barrio Granada, six kilometers east of Bacolod City; and like the rest of the evacuees, we did nothing but dined and guessed on the next move the Japanese Army would take. We learned of the Japanese Army consuming desire at bagging every member of the USAFFE who refused to surrender and we received reports of the increasing number of the Surrenderees as well as their alarming fate once they were inside the Japanese Army prison cells; so I kept on planning on my next courses of action, but I got no chance of implementing any of them because Katchumbo Togue was rescued from the USAFFE stockade and he gathered his children from Barrio Granada and transferred them to Bacolod City. The Tanaka's, the close family friends went with them and I was lumped among the Tanaka family members. Mereza Tanaka took great pains in removing frantically all the red stripes from my military uniforms and all vestiges of my membership to the USAFFE were buried away. I posed as a civilian and I tugged along with the Japanese family.

Mereza Tanaka, in her seventeen's, exuded beauty and youth. The oriental features of her Filipino mother and Japanese father blended in perfect harmony and gifted her with fair skin and delicate complexion. Her oval faces alternated from paleness to rosy color when blood rushed to her veins. Mereza was a picture of innocence and the Japanese Soldiers never missed a visit to her home; and they courted Mereza. Jiro, a Japanese Soldier and one of the most ardent of her suitors, frequented her house and showered her with gifts. Jiro, oftentimes, brought along with him other Japanese Soldiers, and bottles of *sake*[15] and they all went into drinking sprees. Mereza introduced me, as a friend

---

15. Japanese wine.

of her family, to the Japanese Soldiers; so the Japanese Soldiers invited me into joining in their revelry. The invitation presented an opportunity for me of studying the Japanese Soldiers in a face-to-face confrontation and the observation, at close range, of their behavior. I was thinking that the Japanese Army might arrest me during the party in Mereza's house; and I wanted an upper hand, an escape from their capture. I was also thinking of finding out ways of saving my comrades from the Japanese Army prisons, should one was captured. I sampled the Japanese wine as a matter of adjustment; although I was on guard all the time, and I feigned drowsiness when more bottles of wine were emptied while the Japanese Soldiers went into high spirits; so I grabbed an opportunity of studying them more closely. I wondered to myself how the Japanese Soldiers would signal for an arrest of a USAFFE soldier, how they would effect arrest, how they would betray their suspicions, how could a USAFFE Soldier elude the capture, and how could a captive escape the hold of the Japanese Soldiers. These questions kept on nagging me; and I needed immediate answers.

I pretended drunkenness and I inquired nonchalantly from Jiro, the Japanese Soldier who was my rival to Mereza's hand.

"Suppose you see a USAFFE Soldier, what will you do to him?" I asked Jiro who had a working knowledge of the English language.

"Krr!" the Japanese Soldier shouted (meaning "kill") indicating death by rifle shot.

"Suppose," I persisted, "you capture a USAFFE Soldier, what will you do to him?"

"Krrr! Krrr!" chorused the Japanese Soldiers, their hands slashing their throats, as a gesture of death by beheading.

"Suppose," I badgered them, "your friend is a USAFFE Soldier, will you arrest him?"

"Krrr! Krrr! Krrr!" emphasized the Japanese Soldiers in their bold display of loyalty to their country.

"Am I your friend?" I asked and I paused for effect. They all nodded in agreement. "Will you arrest me?"

"No! No!" the Japanese Soldiers disclaimed.

"You will not arrest me?" I faked a mock surprise. "I am a US-AFFE Soldier," I further averred.

"No! No! No!" all the Japanese Soldiers maintained. "You no 'SAPE'!" The Japanese Soldiers meant that they never believed I was a Soldier of the USAFFE.

Figure 4 showed a predicament of a young lady attending to both the USAFFE soldiers and the Japanese Soldiers in a drinking spree.

I was amused into laughter at the situation where I admitted my membership to the United States Armed Forces in the Far East, the Japanese Army quarry, while the Japanese Soldiers denied I was ever a Soldier of the USAFFE.

Franco Villafranca and Fabian Nelda were USAFFE Soldiers while Federico Deslate was an auto mechanic of the Southern Motors with whom I dealt with on matters pertaining to the Military Motor

Pool problems before the Japanese Forces landed in Bacolod City. The three men who became my close friends approached me and urged me into joining them hiding in the mountains. I manifested my indifference to their propositions; instead I broached a plan of surrender to the Japanese Army Headquarters. The trio knew me too well so they declined my idea of surrender; they pleaded for our escape from Bacolod City and mount a resistance against the Japanese Army. I wanted a test of their seriousness and courage; so I brought them along with me to Mereza's house where we attended the session with the Japanese Soldiers. We left the house after the session, but the three men swore that their hair stood on ends during the meeting, and they pledged before we parted, that they would never attend again another meeting with the Japanese Soldiers.

Through the recommendations of Jiro and other Japanese Soldiers, the Japanese Army employed Mereza as Cashier of the University Club, a Japanese nightclub at San Juan Street along the seashore of Bacolod City, and a half-kilometer from Mereza's house in Gonzaga Street. I fetched Mereza from the Club after her night's shift; and on several instances I caught the Japanese Soldiers flirting with her, so I warned Mereza that I would shoot it out with the Japanese Soldiers if they continued their courtship. The Japanese Soldiers invited Mereza, on weekends, to picnics and dances while I followed them from behind with enviousness, which resulted, into lover's quarrels.

I succeeded at keeping my identity as a Soldier of the USAFFE; but the Japanese Army's intensified search for more Soldiers of the USAFFE alarmed me. The suspects were accosted, arrested, interrogated, and incarcerated if they were ever lucky at dodging the Japanese Army death sentences. An entry of a Filipino, a mutual friend, into a love triangle with Mereza, endangered my disguise for once that man who spied for the Japanese Army, detected my romantic link to Mereza, he would, without a shadow of doubt, deliver me to the Japanese Army. My other pitfall was Mereza's and another mutual friend, a lady who frequented Mereza's house and who I discovered was a sympathizer of the Japanese Army. The presence of a *tuba*[16] gatherer who lived next door to Mereza's house and whose wife was a governess to a Japanese National, added to my uneasiness. I felt that the noose of my unmasking as a USAFFE Soldier by the Japanese Army was tightening around my neck. I broached a plan of bringing Mereza along with me to wherever I hid; but Mereza objected to my suggestions. She was the breadwinner of the family after her father's death and she had no heart of leaving her aged mother, young sisters and brothers. I saw the merits of Mereza's objections, but I insisted that she left her employment with the University Club and Mereza obliged with my request by transferring her employment with the Taiwan Trading Company, a Japanese commercial firm.

I delved deeper, time after time, into the motivations of Federico, Fabian and Franco, as I pointed out to them the precarious life of a fugitive. A whole night's sleep might be impossible because we would be on the run most of the time. There might not be shelter shielding us from the sultry heat of the sun, neither from the drenching chilliness of the rain, nor from the incipient hazards of the cold front. We would be left to the mercy of natural elements; and loneliness, discouragement, and the dubiousness of our cause might becloud our vision of freedom. Subsistence would be our paramount concern, and the experience I gained from handling the General Depot illustrated the indispensability of food supply and a need for deep reservoir of forbearance in stockpiling the necessities. We must never discount the possible shifts in the loyalties of many of our comrades and countrymen, for flimsy reason, who might doom our undertakings to failure even from the very beginning; and contemplating that the four of us were up against the well-equipped, fully-armed 16,000 Japanese Soldiers in Negros Islands, was a quixotic misadventure in the face of stark reality. I coaxed my friends into giving us up to the Japanese Army and indulged in a life of ease, comfort, and luxury in the City. The three men remained unfazed against my insistent plea; and their determination sparked me into taking stock of the circumstances facing us.

---

16 Coconut sap.

The piece-meal surrender of the USAFFE Soldiers infuriated the Japanese Army without end; their anger stoked the ember of their zeal in tracking down the renegades. The disorganization that overtook the Negros Islands Defenders abetted the USAFFE Soldiers' dilemma, while the ensuing confusion whetted the Japanese Army appetite in hunting down the recalcitrant. The main thoroughfares of Bacolod City were sealed for several reasons: firstly, because the Japanese Army wanted the recapture of the USAFFE prisoners who bolted the Japanese Army stockade; secondly, because the Japanese Army believed that many of USAFFE Soldiers were holed in the City, hiding under the cloaks of the civilians; and lastly, because the Japanese Army screened every commuter with the mission of bagging every prey. The five-kilometer radius distant from our position to the last Japanese Sentry was virtually a no-man's-land for any USAFFE Soldier. I figured out, by law of averages, that venturing out into the last Japanese Army checkpoint, the possibility of encountering the Japanese Soldiers was ten times to a zero chance of not meeting any one of them. I visualized the ritual before each Japanese Sentry; the commuters were lined up, in single file, before the Japanese Soldiers whose rifles were fixed with bayonets and the Japanese Soldiers barked orders in Japanese language, which the Filipinos hardly understood. The confused front liner, uncomprehending not a word of Japanese, faltered and fumbled until the annoyed Japanese Sentries slapped him at his faces, kicked him or butted him with rifles until he got the message that the garbled instructions were orders for him into saluting the Japanese Guards. The front liner bowed meekly until another command ordered him closest to the Japanese Soldiers. He was frisked all over his body; his belongings searched and emptied into the ground for minute scrutiny. It was his misfortune if a weapon or anything associated with armaments was discovered in his possession for death by bayonet or execution by rifle shot awaited him. The Japanese Army never observed the protocol of war; and the Filipino Civilians were treated harshly and inhumanely almost like they were war combatants. The Filipino Civilians were maltreated, abused, and in most cases executed to death at the slightest displeasure that the Japanese Soldiers in-

curred of them. An escape from the Japanese Army cordon around
Bacolod City seemed almost impossible. The eagle-eyed Japanese
soldiers who were positioned around the Sentry checkpoint were
reserved for those who fled; the Japanese Soldiers were prepared
for the chase or a rain of bullets from their mounted machineguns.
A final yell of "Grr" was a go-signal and goaded the beleaguered
front liner past the demarcation line between life and death, with
beads of perspiration streaking down his faces as signs of relief. I did
not have much time left for more speculation for the imperative of
flight from the City propelled me into swift action before the Japanese Army unraveled my pretenses; therefore, I set my plan into
motion. The four of us crawled around the abandoned USAFFE
Depot, under cover of darkness, and we shoveled the spots I indicated to my three companions. We retrieved the containers of the
stashed arsenals and we logged as many weapons and ammunitions
as we could carry to the house of Mereza, where we assembled four
.45 Cal. Pistols after cleaning them of linseed oil preservatives, for
our immediate use. We padded our pockets with bullets and hand
grenades and stuffed the rest of the weapons in sacks and bags as we
prepared for a break through the Japanese Army Cordon. We were
fully aware of the risks we were taking and the possibility of a shoot-
out with the Japanese Army was a high probability. The reward of
freedom and liberty from the clutches of the Japanese Army far outweighed the risks that we were about to undertake.

We commenced our hegira late past midnight when prying eyes
were fast asleep and darkness joined us in a conspiracy. Instead of
taking the main road five kilometers south from our position and
turning east at the Bacolod City airstrip straight to our destination;
we opted for the least traveled and the shortest route. We utilized
the abandoned railways of the Bacolod-Murcia Sugar Central to
Sitio Mansiliñgan because the railroad bridges facilitated our trek
over steep-bank creeks. Our steps were hurried but our gaits were
subdued for we had resolved that we would never betray the contents of the sacks slung over our shoulders. We repeated our *modus
operandi* over and over again, each time with finesse and a heavy sigh
of relief: speeding up our pace before each Japanese Sentry; slowing

down our tempo for catching our breath before the next Japanese Guard; walking calmly under the noses of the Japanese Sentinels; and before we knew it, we were past the last Japanese Checkpoint!

We paused for a while in deep reflection, for we had many things to be grateful of. We thanked Mereza for seeing us through the Japanese Sentries, although she managed only before the last Japanese Guards, fearful that I might abduct her and bring her along with me. We thanked Mereza's brothers, the Tanaka boys, for theirs was the onus of distracting the attention of the Japanese Soldiers should a worst scenario happened in the Japanese Checkpoint. We valued highly the efforts they expended, many days before our escape, monitoring the Japanese Army movements on the routes we had chosen. It was through the boys' keen observations and comprehensive reports that we unlocked the secret gate through the Japanese Army corridors of checkpoints. We discovered the thin, gray line, which separated night from day, and the moments when the Japanese Soldiers succumbed to the weaknesses of their flesh and their spirits. It was also the time, in an early morning, when cattle dealers scouted stocks for the day's slaughtering businesses; and we mingled with the meat vendors and posed as butchers with bags over our shoulders intended for swine or poultry purchases. We passed by under the very noses of the Japanese Guards who were lulled to sleep by the drowsiness at dawn. The four of us were finally on the road to freedom as we set our course eastward, unaware of the ordeals that awaited us at the other side of the War Zone.

**Figure 5 sketched the recovery of arms and ammunitions
from the abandoned USAFFE Depot.**

CHAPTER 3

Resistance

We set on foot to Murcia, an isolated town, and seventeen kilometers east of Bacolod City. This lowly town of 15,000 brave souls once staged an uprising against the Spanish Regime for the Spanish Government injustices and abuses. The *Pulahan*[17] wrested control of the town until the Spanish Civil Guards drove them to the mountains; and deprived of economy, the valiant Insurgents buckled down into submission in a punitive war of attrition.

When viewed from the air, the town of Murcia spread like a flying falcon with its bill pointing west towards Bacolod City; its right wing pointed north; the forked tail abutted, eastward, the Marapara Mountains and the Canlaon Mountains; while the left span bordered Bago, another municipality of the Province. The burg proper was a rectangle with its main approach from Bacolod City, slicing into Rizal Street, its main thoroughfare, almost at the center of the *poblacion*[18]. The poblacion had an area of a couple of square kilometers with four exit roads; the north road drove a couple of kilometers to Hacienda Binitin, another two kilometers to Hacienda Carmen, five kilometers more to Barrio Granada and six kilometers to Bacolod City; the northeast road

---

17 Red-uniform-wearing Insurgents.

18. Spanish town center.

led to Barrio Alegria, a gateway to the Marapara Mountains; the southeast national highway led to the Canlaon Mountains; and the south national road entered Barrio Cansilayan on its way to the farm lands of the Municipality of Bago.

The town rectangle was so elevated that traffic was discernible kilometers away from all direction. Right after the town plaza, the road sloped abruptly to Lañgub Creek and up to Hacienda Binitin. Enemies coming from the north were visible long before ever reaching the creek and launching an attack against the town. The northeast outlet reclined towards Barrio Alegria before the ascent to the Marapara Mountains; and the route was a vent for a retreating army to the safety of the jungle from a strategic point of view. At the southeastern side of the town, the National Highway dipped before rising to the Canlaon Mountains; and similarly, the path ended into the sanctuary of the forests. The lane to Barrio Cansilayan reclined for kilometers and the road exposed any attacking force against the Town from the south. The main exit was a depression towards Bacolod City and the sight of the Japanese Army convoys rallied the Defenders before the hostile forces ever touched the Town Square. In fact, excavations pockmarked the poblacion when diggings progressed under houses, behind bamboo and orchard trees. Timber planks, bamboo poles and coconut tree trunks were slatted over the pits; and coconut husks and banana stalks reinforced the caverns. The Town seemed defensible for the town people improvised air-raid shelters in anticipation of the Japanese Forces aerial bombardments.

Months earlier, the town folks were kept abreast of war developments. Filipino Soldiers who landed in Bataan supposedly on war exercises etched rosy pictures of the frontlines; to allay fears of his doting parents, a Filipino Soldier with an Artillery Division sent home to his parents an example of a 3-inch circumference, 2-feet long, red painted, and empty cannon shell. The shipment was made in February 1942; thereafter, the tragic news report filtered home. The mighty Japanese Forces attacked and the American and Filipino Defenders were vastly outnumbered and outgunned; as waves after waves of Japanese Soldiers assaulted the defenses of the Filipino and American battlefield positions and the Defenders proved of no match to the onslaught of the invincible Japanese Forces. The Japanese Forces displayed their might in sea, air and land; the Japanese employed their warships, warplanes, tanks and infantry with weaponry of the most advanced technology at the time and crushed the resistance offered by the Defenders. There were shortages of food and ammunitions and the war situation became irreversible. The Filipino and American Soldiers made last-ditch stands but the Japanese Forces overran any resistance put up by the Defenders by sheer power of the number of combat soldiers and the power of weaponry; therefore, the Defenders surrendered.

Thousands of USAFFE Soldiers died along the way, during the Death March on foot from Bataan, a town in Zambales Province to Tarlac, capital of Tarlac Province a distance of approximately 100 kilometers, because any breakaway, from the column for food or water, resulted to an on-the-spot execution. Filipino Civilians, who stood by the roadside and offered food to the prisoners, were driven away; the prisoners were forbidden from accepting food on pain of death. Prisoners, who tired, got exhausted or slowed down in their steps due to hunger, were bayoneted or shot to death by the Japanese Soldiers who marched on relays along and guarded the column of the Death March. Life for the Filipino-American Soldiers held prisoners by the Japanese Forces in Camp O'Donnell (Japanese Army Concentration Camp in Dao) in Capas town, Province of Tarlac, was at its worst with the prisoners cramped in limited spaces and surrounded with barbed wires. There was neither enough food nor was there a regular schedule of meager food rations; therefore, many tried surviving on grasses and even on green residue from animal dung. It was a situation where every one was to his own; there was no quarter given for generosity. The Japanese Concentration Camp was so crowded and unsanitary that many died of sickness and hunger. There was keen competition for survival among prisoners with others stealing every bit of edible items secreted on the person of another; one prisoner choked to death another for a bit of sugar in the latter's possession and another prisoner denied his co-prisoner a sip of water from the former's possession. The result was more deaths for those who had lesser stamina and those whose luck ran out.

News reports of the Japanese Army infamy permeated the minds of the town people that they scampered into all directions when the Japanese Forces landed in Negros Islands on May 22, 1942; and they concluded that the one-aperture air-raid shelters were nothing but death traps against the advancing Japanese Army foot Soldiers. Morbid fears prevailed upon the minds of the town people that a mere scream of *hipon*[19] by an ambulant fish vendor, which rhymed with the word *hapon*[20] dispersed, like spilled beans, the population into all directions. The marketers, who mistakenly heard the word "*habon*"[21] for the word "hapon", while they shopped for goods in the marketplace, scampered in confusion. Thieves profited from the misery of others by warning the town people of the approaching Japanese Army with a shout of "Hapon! Hapon! Hapon!" The town population panicked and left their homes in confusion; and the thieves carted away their valuables before the hoax was exposed.

These were the prevailing scenario when I entered the town of Murcia in June 1942; and I boarded with Gloria Gubaton and transferred later to the house belonging to the family of the Makilan sisters in order that I did not deplete the resources of my hostesses, and in fact, I transferred from one house to the other. My favorite haunt, during daytime, was the marketplace where town dwellers converged, idling their time, exchanging pleasantries or discussing the latest events of the war. I sampled as many varied opinion as I could muster and assessed the attitudes of the town people towards the Japanese Army. I solicited the advice of my uncle, Teodorico Garagara, an old-time resident of the town and whose descendant, Martin Garagara was the founder and the first *presidente*[22] of Murcia. My uncle's children contracted marriages with other residents of the town that I acquired close affinity with the town residents. I con-

---

19. Tiny shrimps.
20. Japanese.
21. Soap.
22. Town Mayor during the Spanish Regime.

sulted all of my relatives, secured their consensus; and I concluded that 99½ % of the town population favored resistance against the Japanese Army. The rest wavered or kept their options to themselves. I started the recruitment of men whom I thought were capable and willing allies in a campaign against the Japanese Forces.

Eulogio Cañonaso joined me; he was of medium build with curly hair but his friendly demeanor belied his courage. He was a bus driver of the defunct Negros Transportation, and as such he knew many of the town residents who were bus passengers.

Jose Lo added to my emerging group. Jose Lo was of Chinese ancestry, of medium height, but his mongoloid faces masked a strong will.

Jose Diaz swelled the number of my band. He was a son of a World War I veteran; his mien veiled toughness and determination.

Eliezer Garagara sided with me. He was short, stocky and muscular. He had thorough knowledge of Bago River and his skills were put later to good use.

The eight of us formed the nucleus of a Guerrilla Band, which left the town and searched for suitable hideout among the rugged terrain. We took advantage of the intervening months, between the Japanese Army landings in Bacolod City and the setting up of their Military Post in Murcia, when the Japanese Army left the town of Murcia alone for a while; while they strengthened their control of Bacolod City, although the Japanese Army patrolled, occasionally, the town of Murcia.

The kite-shaped, fork-tailed map of Murcia was a fascinating contrast in color, were the boundaries of the town defined, colored and pasted together like bits of a jigsaw puzzle. The right wing of the falcon-like shaped town was composed of Barrio Alegria, Barrio Sta. Cruz, Barrio Buenavista, and Barrio Canlandog. The bill belonged to Barrio Blumentritt which main portion merged with Barrio Cansilayan, Barrio Talotog, and Barrio Iglawan for the left wing. Barrio Salvacion, Barrio Abo-abo, Barrio Lopez Jaena, Barrio Caliban, and Barrio Sta. Rosa comprised the body; while Barrio Amayco, Barrio Pandanon and Barrio Igmayaan combined into a tail; and Barrio San Miguel and Barrio Menoyan formed the other.

The town residents surged to the source of Magsuñgay River, at the northern part of the town, which weaned Barrio Blumentritt from Barrio Sta. Cruz, and glided down finally, west to Guimaras Strait in Bacolod City. Magsuñgay River at Barrio Alegria and Barrio Sta. Cruz was a watershed and a source of potable water that supplied the town. The white pebbles and mud less sedimentation of the river were indications of clean, clear, flowing water, which offered sanitation in a healthful environment and a haven from the Japanese Army. Sum-ag River, on the other hand, sprang from Barrio Salvacion and separated Barrio Blumentritt from Barrio Talotog, cut into Barrio Cansilayan before the river settled down to Barrio Sum-ag, a southern village of Bacolod City along the Guimaras Strait. Except for short stretches of Sum-ag River at Barrio Cansilayan where the cliffs were precipitous, the Japanese Army easily crossed the river in pursuit of the Guerilla Soldiers. Guinaman River in the northern "forked tail" of the town partitioned Barrio Buenavista from Barrio Canlandog and Barrio Iglawan from Barrio Lopez Jaena before merging with Bago River, attracted the sturdiest of the evacuees for the steep banks of the river dissuaded the faint-hearted as well as slowed down Japanese Army advances towards the Marapara Mountains and the Canlaon Mountains. Tayuman River, still in the north, isolated Barrio Sta. Rosa from Barrio Amayco before the river entered Barrio Sta. Rosa and branched into Poncian River and Tayuman River; Poncian River sequestered Barrio Lopez Jaena from Barrio Sta. Rosa before both rivers emptied into Bago River. These rivers attracted sizeable numbers of evaders from the Japanese Army as the waterways offered hindrances to the Japanese Army use of vehicles in pursuit of their enemies. The fleers slipped to as far as Talos River that traversed the boundaries of Barrio Pandanon and Barrio Igmayaan, the last frontiers of the town in the north. After Talos River, the ascent to the Marapara Mountains began where the ravines were so stiff that a traveler's chin touched his knees while he negotiated the canyons. Asia

River and Pula River that tumbled down, in parallel, from Canlaon Mountains past Barrio Menoyan and Barrio San Miguel in
their flow towards Bago River, amassed evacuees from the town
eastward to the mountains. Bago River, the largest and the lon-
gest River in Negros Islands, offered a natural barrier against
the onslaught of the Japanese Army. Bago River sprang from
the mountainside of Marapara Mountains, northeast of Murcia,
and winded its way down to the town of Bago before the river merged with Guimaras Strait. The source of Bago River appeared from a distance like a figure of a white stallion embedded to a wall of a mountain; in fact the place where Bago River
originated was oftentimes referred to as "kolokabayo" which
meant "horse-like". Bago River flowed down from Marapara
Mountains, southwest along the fringes of Barrio Pandanon,
and crossed over to the Canlaon Mountains along the edges of
Barrio Menoyan and Barrio San Miguel where a couple of kilometers down the Barrio, Bago Ferry Mambucal Bridge forded
Bago River. Bago River parted Barrio San Miguel from Barrio
Lopez Jaena on its way past Barrio Iglawan and Barrio Cansilayan before shifting southwest to Barrio Maao of Bago town
before it belonged to Guimaras Strait.

The people who sensed the impending initial arrival of the
Japanese Army went into hiding to the different places of the
town. They congregated under the *pawâ*[23] trees teeming on riverbanks along the waterways; and devised Quonset huts out of the
pawâ trees, which they cut to sizes and tied them together with
rattan twines. The makeshifts were neatly tucked under the canopies of the thick, willowy reeds; and they served as living quarters,
sleeping, dining, parlor game hall and salon for passersby who
regaled the occupants with tales of their sporadic victories over
the Japanese Army. Reports of guerrilla ambuscades mounted
against the Japanese Patrol in Barrio Sum-ag, Barrio Abuanan,
Barrio Mining, and Barrio Iglawan, filtered to evacuation places as far as Asia River banks, and as early as the Japanese Army

23. Specie of thorn less bamboo tree.

ventured out of Bacolod City. The news reports were heartening
to the evacuees who believed that the Filipinos had a fighting
chance of repulsing the Japanese Army, anticipating that with reports of their brutalities they inflicted on the Filipino prisoners in
Luzon, the Filipino Civilians would be spared of cruelties of their
occupation. The tale bearers were often rewarded with hearty
meals in appreciation for their grapevine services; the listeners
believed that they were remnants of the disbanded USAFFE who
were bidding for appropriate time in mounting resistance to the
Japanese Forces. The dwellings were concealed from the Japanese warplane reconnaissance by building them under tall trees
on the valleys; the occupants were prohibited from setting fire
for whatever purpose; or else the smoke betrayed the presence
of the civilians in the area, to the Japanese warplane pilots who
reported to the Japanese Army ground forces. The Japanese
Army Patrol Soldiers efficiently located the convergence of the
Filipino Civilians.

The Japanese Army exerted concerted efforts in attracting the
people back to the town; and the people acquiescence was based
more on life necessities than on fear of the Japanese soldiers.
The Japanese Army did not immediately settle in the town; the
Japanese Patrol staged sporadic raids, which drove the people
back to hiding until the Japanese Soldiers were gone. It was just
like a game of cat-and-mouse between the population and the
Japanese Army in the initial stage of the war. Scenarios occurred
whenever the Japanese Patrol entered the town accompanied
by gun fires announcing their unexpected arrivals; people panicked and hid their heads like ostriches and unaware that their
bottoms were exposed, some wiggled out of tight spots at record
time that defied duplication, and another rode on a horse, beat
frantically the stallion but forgetting that the horse was still tied
securely to the stable.

The Japanese Army established finally a Garrison in the town
of Murcia, and they coaxed the town people into coexistence
with the Japanese Soldiers. Commerce sprang back quickly and
especially near the Garrison, the municipal building and the

town public plaza. The Japanese Soldiers held their morning rituals of praying at the rising sun and mass calisthenics every morning. A Japanese Lieutenant and a Soldier staged a duel with the use of wooden poles; thrusting poles against each other when the Soldier accidentally thrust below the belt of the Lieutenant who screamed in extreme agony; but the Japanese Lieutenant took, good-naturedly, the accidental blow. Japanese Soldiers oftentimes exhibited skill and courage by balancing themselves walking on the edges of the roof around the 50-foot tall municipal building. The Japanese Soldiers encouraged sports and they played basketball games against the Filipino Civilians, unaware that their opponents like Josefino Calansiñgin, Nicolas Alit, Etat Villarosa, Romeo Villarosa, Jose Alit and many others, were Guerrilla Intelligence Operatives. The basketball players relayed secret messages on the disposition and movements of the Japanese Army in the Garrison. Many civilians were spared of death whenever the Japanese Army sent out Patrols because the guerrilla operatives relayed, in advance, notice to the Filipino Civilians along the Japanese Patrol paths.

The Japanese Army engaged in farming; in the production of ramie and cotton. They converted hectares of Riceland and sugar cane fields into ramie and cotton plantations; plowing the fields, planting ramie seedlings and cotton seedlings, cultivating, fertilizing, and spraying the plants with insecticides. The agricultural operations required intensive employment of labor and the Japanese Army harnessed the Filipino Civilians. Japanese civilian agricultural Supervisors led the Filipinos to the farm sections in the performance of specific agricultural operation, and oftentimes the Filipino workers were caught idling which infuriated the Japanese who meted punishments by slapping the faces of the lazy-bones. The farm activities went on for a while with the Japanese Supervisors becoming sterner in their discipline of the workers; until another Guerrilla Band kidnapped Yasda, a Japanese plantation supervisor, during his round of inspection. The short-lived agricultural venture ceased when the Filipino workers deserted the Japanese plantations, knowing fully well that the

Japanese Army would exact retributions from the remaining laborers as their scapegoats; as a consequence the Japanese Army became more violent in their dealings with the Filipino Civilians and the Filipinos distanced as far away as possible from the Japanese Army and the town.

Stripped of the sugar cane plantations, the environs of Murcia was an even balding piece of earth; so we never had a chance of hiding near the town from the Japanese Army who possessed heavy weapons, motorized vehicles and war planes that pinpointed our positions. We moved south and pitched camp at Barrio Abuanan with Barrio Cansilayan serving as a buffer zone against the Japanese Army coming from the town of Murcia. Barrio Cansilayan was a row of houses along unpaved streets and the luxuriant bamboo trees that grew on backyards and along the streets concealed our movements. The steep banks of Sum-ag River offered a natural barrier but the abandoned railroad bridge still allowed the entry of the Japanese Patrol to Barrio Cansilayan, so we posted riflemen in our side of the bridge challenging any Japanese Army incursion into our area. We selected Barrio Abuanan as our training ground because of its propinquity to Murcia, Barrio Sum-ag, and Sitio Crossing Mining, another exit way to the south of Barrio Cansilayan; but above all other considerations, we chose Barrio Abuanan because it adjoined Bago River which we crossed to a sanctuary in the mountains.

I saw the urgent need for the formation of a strike force so we could launch counter-attacks before the Japanese Army swooped down on us and nipped the buds of our clandestine war preparations. Gaudencio Claridad, a barrio elder, who became my armory custodian, assisted in manpower recruitment; although, in a small locality like Barrio Abuanan, our doings never escaped notice and people flocked to us for curiosity's sake. The kind of occupation that an applicant engaged in did not matter in consideration for entrance to our group, nor the lack of military expertise diminished his chance of admission; but I picked men with qualities that would ensure the success of experimentation in guerrilla warfare. I discouraged affiliation of those with doubtful motivations for I disapproved of the utilization of the organization for self-aggrandizement. Many applicants were rejected for I was selective in the choice of membership; and I visited the recruit's home in an effort of probing deeper into the candidate's sources of income as well as his style of living and family inter-relationships. After an applicant was admitted, he underwent apprenticeship until his demeanor warranted the grant of firearms; and I ensured that he passed the test for perseverance, loyalty, and patriotism. Many of my recruits were marginal landowners around the barrios, who continued farming in support of their families while they fought for country and freedom.

Standing roughly in the midst of 150 men culled from the greenest of the tyros, I recalled the many combat lessons that I had studied from the General Military Troop School. The USAFFE Soldiers in the group led the mass exercises.

Feet set apart.

Rifle butt rested squarely against the shoulder.

Rifle placed at shoulder level.

Gun sight aligned.

"Anticipate the reaction of bullets leaving the nozzle of gun barrel," I cautioned the trainees. .

Adjust your grips and make allowances for the kick."

"Aim at your targets."

"When you are ready, press the trigger and fire."

I brought along with me lemon fruits and handed two to each cadet.

"Squeeze the lemon fruits slowly but firmly," I instructed them.

"Assume that the lemon fruits were gun triggers," I demonstrated crushing the lemon fruits effectively. Then I substituted the lemon fruits with the gun triggers.

"Now, squeeze the gun trigger slowly but firmly," I coached them.

"Squeeze the trigger the way you squeezed the lemon fruits!"

My patience was taxed to the limit but the results were beyond my expectations; for the cadets learned the fundamentals and they became prepared for the defense of their territory.

I retrieved a truckload of arm cache from the caves where I stashed them earlier; the caves hollowed by an abandoned Jolo Sugar Mill, the site of an olden crude sugar central that operated during the Spanish Era, at Hacienda Esmeralda, past the irrigation lines at Barrio Cansilayan, which abutted Bago River, opposite the plateau of Sitio Sandiñgaw of Bago town; and I distributed the arms to my men. We had 75 Enfield rifles, 8 Garands with 8 grenade launchers, and 2 Browning Automatic Rifles with 8 magazines. We possessed 18 .45 Cal. Pistols with 16 magazines with complete ammunitions, 5 boxes of hand grenades and 45 boxes of live ammunitions for the rifles. The banks of Bago River reverberated with barks of guns as culmination rite to our training exercises; the rest of the apprentices served as non-combatant support group.

The Japanese Army landed in Bacolod City in May 1942, before I left Bacolod City the following month and arrived in Murcia in June while we completed our guerrilla training two months later in August when the Japanese Army was still concentrated in Bacolod City except for their sporadic raids to places around Bacolod City including the town of Murcia. We were at Barrio Abuanan, a center of the road curvature that originated west from Bacolod City, 17 kilometers east to the town of Murcia, 7 kilometers south to Barrio Cansilayan, 2 kilometers more to Barrio Abuanan, and the road changed direction west 5 kilometers to Barrio Sum-ag, and finally north 9 kilometers back o Bacolod City.

We moved around Barrio Abuanan, a rice granary and other land areas surrounded by rice lands of Barrio Cansilayan, Barrio Sumag, and south to include Crossing Mining of Bago town, and we tried our campaign lines on landowners for support to our budding Guerrilla Band. We urged the landowners into the production of more food while they shared with us their production for the subsistence of my Guerrilla Band, and my Soldiers fought the Japanese Army in protection of their life and property. I was extremely elated and encouraged when a landowner handed me his Sedan as his expression of support. Federico Deslate who was an expert auto mechanic went to work; he made alterations on the automobile carburetor and the car ran on gasoline, alcohol or kerosene whichever fuel was available. We hang a Filipino flag on one side of the automobile and an American flag on the other side, in our efforts at drumming up the spirit of patriotism among our supporters as well as boosting our morale. The vehicle kept us mobile and we took advantage of speed as we ventured further to Barrio Sumag where we disseminated our crusade, and reaped heartening results. Elpidio Macasa and Tomas Abdon, both residents of Barrio Sumag and the men who proved later on their toughness, joined my Guerrilla Band. Isidro Villarosa, rice landowner in the Barrio, assured me of continued rice supply. Ana Villarosa, another rice landowner pledged voluntary food supply to my troops. Rosario Villarosa, another rice landowner and owner of a fishpond assured me of her support. Hieroteo Villarosa, another landowner in the Barrio and a Lawyer by profession, pledged to me his support; in fact, our ranks swelled when talks of the birth of a Guerrilla Resistance Movement circulated. And as a result, new recruits bolstered my ranks and more assurances of support poured in.

I saw the urgent need for more armaments in accommodation to the enthusiastic and determined volunteers, who multiplied the number of the Guerrilla Band, and I saw the need of entering Bacolod City and recovering more of the arms I secreted around the discarded USAFFE Depot, but more than the need for arms, I wanted a visit to Mereza Tanaka. Friends whom I contacted in Bacolod City condescended grudgingly and arranged for a lunch meeting between Mereza Tanaka and me in her house at Gonzaga Street. My Japanese Army Counter Spy facilitated my four other trusted men and my entry, and Mereza's mother reassured me that a note had been passed on to Mereza for a meeting after her work break from Taiwan Trading Company. The long hours of waiting slipped by without Mereza coming home, and the failure of the meeting disappointed me so much, but it turned out that Mereza was fearful of my presence in the City and my capture by the Japanese Army; so I vented my frustrations by digging deeper into the storage for more weapons. My companions and I loaded the weapons into caretellas and retraced our routes into a fast exit. It might have been a pure coincidence but the lodging houses, which we occupied at our entry point, were smoldering ashes when we came back; the Japanese Patrol razed the structures to the ground minutes after our entry passage.

I rejoined my Outfit at Barrio Vista Alegria, a barrio a couple of kilometers from Gonzaga Street of Bacolod City, and we marched in column eastward to Hacienda Oliva, a sugar cane plantation located between Bacolod City and the town of Murcia. The Filipino Civilians whom we passed by along our way, stared blankly at us for they never comprehended our real identity, and gawked at us for they marveled at the sight of a column of well-armed Filipinos in civilian attire, parading inside an enemy territory. I led the Column and I tried avoiding the stares of as many Filipinos as I encountered while they were on their way into Bacolod City because many of these Filipinos were in cohorts with the Japanese Army; and I wanted my disguise stood a chance of hiding my identity. My attention was distracted, however, when Manuel Palma, one of my Soldiers, signaled me to a stop; so I waited for him while he advanced towards me.

"Will you meet Ramon Javelona?" Manuel inquired with a stocky man in his tow. Ramon Javelona sidled to me and inquired.

"Are you the Jorge Herrera, the leader of a Guerrilla Band?"

I nodded.

"I heard so much about you and your resistance activities; and I am very grateful now that I see you in person."

Ramon Javelona hugged me as I thanked him for his words of encouragement; but I had more tasks waiting ahead of me, so my Column proceeded. Manuel Palma explained later to me that Ramon Javelona got curious of the armed group, and inquiring from Manuel; Ramon Javelona guessed that I skipped his notice for a hunch never crossed his mind that a lean, brown-skinned, and shy 25-year old points' man, was a guerrilla leader.

The farm laborers who were heading towards their shanties greeted our approach at Hacienda Oliva; but the drones of aircrafts superimposed on their attentions and the farmers alerted us. The farmers associated the buzzing of the Japanese Forces aircrafts, from bitter experiences in the past, with the accompanying machinegun fires from the sky, and the least precautionary measures they adopted was lying themselves flat between the separations of the rows of lush sugar cane fields; while we headed for the automobile which we had left behind and hidden in the area. The car engine stalled and the vehicle remained immobile at the time when we wanted most an instant escape from the perils of the Japanese warplane bombardments.

Federico Deslate, the Guerrilla Band auto mechanic, went to work by feverishly pinpointing the errant components of the car; while the rest of us entrenched ourselves in ditches with our rifles trained skyward for aerial counter attack, but the Japanese warplanes flew over us, and missed our armed presence. Federico corrected the problem with our motor vehicle and we completed our trip back to Barrio Abuanan.

We had occasions of displaying proudly the American and Filipino flags which we latched on to both sides of our ash-gray painted automobile. We paraded our automobile around Barrio Sumag, Barrio Abuanan, Barrio Cansilayan, and Murcia when we determined that the Japanese Warplanes were out of the skies. Our presence in the town square of Murcia was greeted by the people with mixed reactions; a majority expressed enthusiasm, others disbelief. A few of the population branded our undertakings foolhardy, but we persisted with our objectives; we campaigned for support, we fathomed the attitude, sincerity, and loyalty of the people, and we wanted the identity of those who would betray our resistance movement. Rosendo Hermosura expressed extreme cynicism against our clandestine maneuvers because he felt that our endeavor was foolhardy and we would never succeed against the well-armed Japanese Army; but I was not surprised because I knew all along that he biked his way at night to Bacolod City where he reported regularly our nefarious activities to the Japanese Army Headquarters. The Japanese Army blockaded our automobile while we were at Barrio Abuanan, but we had removed the American and Filipino Flags, and we had made good our escape, before the Japanese Soldiers set our automobile to flames and razed our vehicle to the ground.

CHAPTER 4

Rivalries

The disbandment of the United States Armed Forces in the Far East in Negros plunged the Islands into utter confusion; uncertainties filled the people's mind, and fears gripped their hearts. Anarchy reared its ugly head for anybody who possessed weapons claimed authority for himself; the gun wielders threw away law and order into the wind, while they exacted allegiance by the barrel of their guns. Guns and bullets stoked their lust for power while illusions blinded their vision for glory. My compatriots, whom I had consulted, viewed my philosophy of armed confrontation against the Japanese Army, as a radical and foolhardy approach to war. Many of my confidants argued that the odds of winning the war my way were stacked overwhelmingly against my favor that drumming for support would never be an easy task. I disagreed with the majority of my friends because I had a mission in my mind. I would teach the Japanese Army an abject lesson that there were Filipino soldiers who were willing and ready to give up their lives for the sake of Country and liberty.

The Japanese Army took time in consolidating their forces in Bacolod City and the dispersal of their soldiers to every town, barrio and village in Negros Islands, and required them several months before they established Garrisons in strategic places. They pursued relentlessly the USAFFE soldiers who remained at large; but more importantly they wanted the cooperation of the Filipino Civilians and in these aspects the Japanese Army approached landowners around the vicinity of Murcia, and assessed whether the people in a hacienda were in favor or against them. The Filipinos easily outsmarted the Japanese Soldiers by answering adeptly their interrogations.

"Are you a USAFFE soldier?" The Japanese interrogators would surprise an individual by catching him off guard with blunt questions.

"No." was a prudent Filipino answer, which appeased the Japanese Soldiers.

"Have you seen USAFFE soldiers?" The Japanese Army loved most a Filipino's admission of seeing USAFFE soldiers, so a Filipino civilian's prudent answer was a, "yes."

"Where are they?" The Filipino's best answer that satisfied most the Japanese Army's Inquisitors was a gesture of pointing towards the mountains, and then the Japanese Soldiers concluded that the Filipino Civilian was telling the truth; admitting, seeing USAFFE soldiers and informing the Japanese Army of their whereabouts.

The Japanese Army, who was unfamiliar of the mountain terrains and fearful of armed USAFFE soldier's ambuscades, never dared a pursuit to the dense forests.

Ildefonso Coscolluela was among the Hacienda owners whom the Japanese Army approached because the Japanese Army wanted the services of his laborers for their agricultural program. "Junior" as his laborers fondly called him, was of medium build, stocky, broad shoulder, and was of Spanish descent, which chose the path of staying with his laborers; instead of residing in Bacolod City as most other landowners did. He was closely attached to his farm workers that, even the arrival of the Japanese Forces did not severe his relationship with them. The Sugar Central stopped milling operations and the sugar canes that were still growing, were left rotting on the fields; thus depriving Ildefonso Coscolluela of income from the usual milling of canes and selling of sugar, the proceeds with which he subsidized his sugar cane plantation. With the stoppage of sugar production, Ildefonso Coscolluela switched to rice production and the Japanese Army located him in his Hacienda Puyas, a couple of kilometers southwest of Murcia, and concluded that Coscolluela and his men were not affiliates of the USAFFE, but farmers; and therefore they left him unmolested except for the surprise visits on his farm land which the Japanese Army conducted occasionally.

In the Philippines, a third world country where the majority of the population lived below poverty line, a land owner like Ildefonso Coscolluela who owned roughly 50 hectares of sugar cane plantation, derived considerable income from the farm land, which classified him as a man of considerable wealth; and therefore, he commanded veneration as dispenser of labor employment. Further more, Hacienda Puyas belonged previously to Jose Domingo whose spouse was my mother's relative; therefore, I was compelled by both nostalgia and an idea of ascertaining the prevailing political atmosphere in the area in relationship with the Japanese Army control. Ildefonso Coscolluela summoned me for a meeting in his Hacienda and I guaranteed his messenger of my presence, in spite of lingering doubts I entertained in my mind of his political leanings. I was not sure of his loyalty to his Country, but I wanted the meeting for ascertaining whether he was collaborating with the Japanese Army; his Hacienda being near the town and the Japanese Army left him alone, or was he in favor of resisting the enemy. I relinquished my troops in Hacienda San Enrique, three kilometers away and I headed north to Hacienda Puyas. Dressed in a pair of short pants and a jacket over my shirts, I carried a pistol and hand grenades; and I silhouetted as a lone figure of a carabao tender walking on ditches and carabao paths as I traveled along the separation lanes of the unharvested sugar canes, until I reached his location. The Langub Creek that flowed past the northern section of the town plaza and crossed the national highway at Barrio Blumentritt a couple of kilometers, west of the town, parted Hacienda Puyas; and Ildefonso Coscolluela had his hacienda house built near the creek that lay in a lower elevation than his farm lands, and his house was hidden by tall trees from view of the national highway.

My knocks at his door brought me in during lunchtime; so Junior invited me to a lunch table.

We discussed the many aspects of the war; its duration which might end shortly or last for years, and the aftermath of the conflict as they affected the Filipino Civilians and the Filipino guerrilla soldiers. It was revealed only after World War II ended that the Japanese Imperial Forces designed the war with the conquest of the Philippines in the shortest time possible, the conscription of the Filipinos into the Japanese Army and the harness of the Philippine resources in the accomplishment of their timetable for the conquest of the neighboring Island of Borneo and other Pacific Islands in the war that Japan waged against the United States. Ildefonso Coscolluela argued that co-operation with the Japanese Army was the most sensible way of protecting the lives and the property of the Filipinos; especially that the United States Armed Forces in the Far East surrender, had signified the hopelessness of a position of armed resistance to the Japanese Imperial Army. I understood his viewpoints and the feeling of Ildefonso Coscolluela because he was a civilian and a farmer who was most concerned with his land and the life of his farm workers; but I was a Soldier who was trained along warfare and loyalty to the Country, so I expressed my disagreement with his position.

We were at the middle of the meal course when one of Ildefonso Coscolluela's laborers barged in haste, and alerted us of the Japanese Patrol's arrival. Ildefonso dropped his silverwares, and looked straight into my eyes, just as I stared blankly back at him. We looked into each other's eyes in a moment of silence, before he found words that broke the spell.

"Jorge, I did not summon you and set you up for entrapment for the Japanese Army," he assured me.

"I know," I replied with a note of apprehension and in a low voice. "We may never get out alive of this place, in any way, if the Japanese Soldiers entered this house." My hands gripped my gun and felt for a hand grenade.

"Gather as many fowls as you can and offer them as gifts to the Japanese Army." Junior instructed his laborers.

I planned, within my mind, an option of a backdoor gate away route and slipped into the sugarcane fields and got lost among the lush greeneries, should the Japanese Patrol headed towards our direction or I shoot it out with them. We monitored the Japanese Soldiers' movements and held our breath as the Japanese Patrol tarried for a while; and then we breathed a sigh of relief when the Japanese Soldiers departed via a different route.

Ildefonso Coscolluela erased any cloud of suspicion of his loyalty to the Country, and inspired by my presentation of a guerrilla resistance plan; he tendered 200 sacks of palay as his pledge of tangible support to my guerrilla movement, which he shipped later to my hideout. Words of these contribution reached Serafin Guacena who was organizing another guerrilla band which claimed a base of operation around the vicinity of the town; therefore, he claimed jurisdiction over the territory including that of Hacienda Puyas, and consequently, he insisted that the 200 sacks of palay dole outs belonged to his guerrilla group. Serafin Guacena spread his claims of ownership through gossips and innuendoes among the residents in the town and the surrounding areas, which eventually reached my knowledge; and in like manner, I registered my objections to his claims because the contributions were donations to my guerrilla band of a friend's volition. There was never any territorial jurisdiction, since there was never a meeting of minds among leaders of the nebulous guerrilla resistance movement; therefore, I never recognized Serafin Guacena's control over the vicinities surrounding the town of Murcia. What started as hearsay claims and counter claims soon developed into vast differences of opinion between us that were fueled by insinuations, egotism and challenges. Bystanders, on both sides of an imaginary fence, who stood at gaining nothing out of our quarrel but personal gratification over an outcome of a duel between two combatants, attributed insults, bravado, dares into each other's camps; and hatred and animosities widened the schism between us. With touched sensibilities, smarted egos and ruffled feelings; we agreed on a confrontation and we girded for a showdown in any place and at anytime we encountered each other.

I chose a Sunday for a confrontation with Serafin Guacena, when I entered Murcia and I betted against me that Serafin Guacena was also in town on market days. I had been trained in the General Military Troop School in the use of a .45 Caliber Automatic pistol that I felt confident I could handle my opponent. There were very few of us who passed the test that the United States Army trainers administered at the end of the training exercises. I could place, on a table, two handguns, and dare my opponent into picking up one of them; if he took the gun with his right hand, I took the other with my left hand, or the other way around. I felt, in any event, that I could shoot faster and hit accurately my target with a shot before my opponent hit me. I hit any target with equal accuracy with the use of either my right or my left hand. My Military Trainers practiced me in twirling the .45 Caliber pistols, after the gun trigger hammer was cocked and the safety pin released, between my thumb and my forefinger. The danger lay when the pistol was rotating and an extra pressure was applied against its trigger, for the pistol went off hitting anybody at the moment the gun barrel was pointing to. Very few of us, the trainees, completed the exercises for only 10 out of every 100 candidates passed the test. The secret lay in applying the right amount of pressure between the thumb and the forefinger against the trigger and the trigger guard while the handgun was rotated.

I knew Serafin Guacena as a casual acquaintance because we both grew up in Bacolod City before World War II broke out; but each of us never fathomed the skills, capabilities, determination and courage of each other. I walked from Lopez Jaena Street, south of the town, and made my way left to Rizal Street. Reports of my appearance traveled fast to the marketplace and the marketers stampeded in panic. The cyclone wire fences that were securely tied to concrete posts around the market square gave way to people who rammed against the enclosures and leveled them to the ground in their desperate flight in avoiding cross fires. I negotiated Rizal Street to the front side of the marketplace with an automatic pistol in my right hand and a reserved magazine clip of bullets in my left hand.

Serafin Guacena was tall, of medium build, and stocky who emerged fully armed, from the opposite direction. The news however, of our impending confrontation shot like an arrow into the air, and in an instant reached Alejandro Montelibano who lived nearby in Hacienda Binitin, his sugar cane plantation, and who arrived in time and interposed himself between me and Serafin Guacena. "Ditong" as he was fondly known around town, appealed to both Guacena's and my senses as he reminded us that nothing good would come out by fighting each other. It was to the best interests of the Filipino Civilians and the Country if we concentrated on fighting the Japanese Army; otherwise the Japanese Army would be the sole beneficiary of the death of two courageous Filipino Guerrilla Leaders. Alejandro "Ditong" Montelibano, a proverbial cooler head, pacified us, patched our differences; and he averted a bloody duel to death.

Serafin Guacena never realized that a night before, my Soldiers entered the town and monitored the movements of all his followers. My Soldiers were behind each of his armed men while others hid behind the large acacia trees that lined along both sides of the Gabaldon-type school buildings that faced the market place across the street. My order to my Soldiers was explicit, "Don't shoot until I was felled down by my opponent's bullet."

Gil Escaro was another Guerrilla Leader who appropriated to himself the area around Barrio Sumag as his guerrilla zone. He invited me to a meeting with the purpose of uniting our groups; and he set up a Sunday for the meeting at Barrio Sumag. I was suspicious of him that I approached the meeting place with caution. The meeting proceeded in festive mood and with gaiety as the supply of native wine enlivened the spirits of all men who participated in the conference. At the appointed time when Gil Escaro's Soldiers got intoxicated, I flashed the prearranged signal, and my Soldiers divested Escaro's followers of all their weapons including a prized knife, which Escaro carried for personal use.

Captain Uriarte, another Guerrilla Leader, from the south sent me feelers after feelers for the purpose of a meeting; he wanted that we combine our forces together against the Japanese Army. I was not sure of his motivation and loyalty; besides, I preferred fighting against the Japanese Army around the town of Murcia from where I earned the support of the population. Captain Uriarte was mounting a resistance movement near Hinigaran, a southern town of the Province with far access to the mountains. I preferred my hideout located near the rugged Canlaon Mountains, with Bago River acting as buffer against the Japanese Army, between my mountain hideouts and rice fields as sources of food supply across the river. Captain Uriarte sent several of his followers after me, inviting me for a conference; but I declined his invitation because I felt that he needed my armory and my followers more than urgency for unity. He finally sent me his most trusted henchmen with instructions of bringing me to him, dead or alive, but I successfully eluded their ruses. It was not uncommon for anyone, who possessed a weapon, getting waylaid, slain and divested of his armament. There was an acute need for weaponry and capable manpower that guerrilla leaders went to all extent at acquiring them. The accretion of guerrilla leaders and the ever changing balance of powers among them caught many civilians in the horns of dilemma; the civilians were torn apart by choices of guerrilla leaders with whom they could entrust with their lives and property.

My Guerrilla Band was enroute to Barrio Cansilayan when Catalino Tenebro, a hacienda overseer, blocked our way; he was in a hurry, he informed us because time was running out for his landlord. Francisco Rojas, another sugar cane plantation owner, remained undecided up to the eleventh hour as to a Guerrilla Leader on whom he would rely with the protection of the lives of his family and his property. Hacienda Paco Rojas, his plantation, was a couple of kilometers south of the town of Murcia, and along the national highway to Barrio Cansilayan. The Japanese Army decreed an ultimatum to Francisco Rojas ordering his surrender at noontime, to the Japanese Army Garrison in the town.

Catalino Tenebro recommended my Guerrilla Band to Francisco Rojas as a shield against the Japanese Army, and Francisco Rojas finally agreed to his Overseer's pleadings. Catalino Tenebro explained to me the predicaments of Francisco Rojas and asked me if I could bail out his Landlord from imminent danger. I acceded to Catalino Tenebro's entreaty; therefore, I advised Francisco Rojas through Catalino Tenebro, his messenger, to bring his family across Bago River to my hideout, while I secured his retreat route from the Japanese Army. At the expiration of the deadline that the Japanese Army gave Francisco Rojas and Rojas' failure of surrender, sixteen truckloads of Japanese Soldiers arrived at his hacienda for the enforcement of the Japanese Army edict, but finding Francisco Rojas gone, the Japanese Soldiers set to flames the houses of Francisco Rojas. Francisco Rojas reported eventually to the Headquarters of Colonel Ernesto Mata who appointed him Supply Officer of Negros Islands Resistance Movement.

Envies, disagreements of opinion and styles of leadership rocked the guerrilla movement with dissensions and rivalries. F/Sgt. Emilio Ermio was also a USAFFE soldier who proceeded to Barrio Abuanan and organized his own guerrilla band. Learning of the existence of my Group, Emilio Ermio proposed to me that we combined our forces, as we both believed that we would gain strength through our unity. I consented to his idea and we collaborated on numerous battle encounters, until insidious divisiveness crept between us.

I treated fairly my Soldiers; sharing equally with all members everything that the group possessed. Aside from leading the group into battlefields, I was nobody but an ordinary soldier like any one of my men. I never enjoyed preferential treatment in food, clothing, and other conveniences; instead, I took good care of every one of them by providing them with food, clothing, cigarettes, medicine, and even with minute household items as I looked after their welfare. After each combat engagement, I assembled them at pre-designated places where food filled their empty stomachs and rest alleviated their weary sinews; and they were always refreshed after each battle encounter.

F/Sgt. Emilio Ermio believed otherwise, and in many instances, he insisted on seniority in military rank and demanded preferential treatment from men under his command. He got the best of everything, while his men contented themselves of the remainder, to which style of leadership, I registered my disapproval; and we headed together into a break up. The straw that broke the camel's back was an incident involving a Browning automatic rifle which I awarded to a loyal supporter for the hacienda Overseer's wholehearted support to my group. Emilio Ermio's men confiscated the prized weapon leading to an altercation between Ermio and me during a confrontation. Resting a revolver on Emilio's shoulder, I threatened him with a blown off ear if he did not confess; so Emilio Ermio admitted responsibility for the confiscation and named the culprits. I hunted the offenders until days of sleuthing paid off when I caught up with them, while they were resting, their rifles stacked neatly nearby, and the men were in the middle of their repasts. Rushing towards them, I caught them rooted to their seats, surprised and perplexed; my Soldiers gathered all the weapons and I recovered the missing Rifle. The culprits begged on joining my Outfit, but I refused because I did not want any part of Emilio Ermio's men. Emilio Ermio's and my path seldom crossed from then on.

Rivalries among Guerrilla Leaders exacted tolls on precious human lives and loss of property; as deceptions, entrapments, and ambushes were employed in the attainment of the possession of weapons, food or control of leadership. Alarmed at the worsening developments that hampered the growth of the fledgling Guerrilla Resistance Movement, Major Ernesto Mata, who assumed later on the rank of Lieutenant Colonel of Negros Islands Resistance Movement, summoned Guerrilla Leaders to a general assembly. It was time for the organization and coordination of efforts of the resistance movement and the formation of a unified Guerrilla Resistance Movement Command. Recognizing the legitimacy of the leadership of Lt. Colonel Ernesto Mata, I affiliated my Guerrilla Band under his leadership and command.

CHAPTER 5

Ambuscades

For over a month since I fled from Bacolod City on June 8, 1942, I concentrated on recruitment, training and procurement of logistics; and the time had come for an encounter with the Japanese Forces as an acid test of our mettle in guerrilla warfare. I wondered to myself if the recruits would stand up squarely and stare bravely at the face of death from every bullet that spewed from enemy guns The recruits had learned the fundamentals of combat, but I wondered if they assimilated all the instructions; the time came for separating the men from the boys and there was no margin for error for a slightest mistake meant instant death. The baptism of fire came on July 29, 1942 when we laid in wait in an ambush.

F/Sgt. Emilio Ermio and I joined forces; and our group of 150 men faced southward. Crossing Mining was six kilometers from our hideout in Barrio Abuanan, and the railroad track that bisected the road between Crossing Mining and Barrio Abuanan favored our battle position; we had many optional routes of escape of either east to the mountains, west along the Bago River or north back to our hideout. We had observed closely that the Japanese Patrol on motor vehicles frequented Barrio Maao because the Barrio was a gateway to the Canlaon Mountains, and the Japanese Army suspected that Guerrilla Soldiers frequented the Barrio. The Japanese Army Soldiers rode on trucks with machine guns mounted on vehicles while they negotiated the distance of 21 kilometers between the town of Bago and Barrio Maao.

Barrio Crossing Mining was shaped like a letter "T" with top sides pointing east to Barrio Maao, and west to Bago town; while the stem of the "T" pointed north to Barrio Abuanan. A creek ran along the road to Barrio Maao and the town of Bago while the road from Barrio Abuanan ended perpendicularly at Crossing Mining. The tall bamboo trees that grew abundantly along the banks of the creek hid conveniently the view of the creek from the road; and the tall bamboo trees as well as large mango trees hid us from the observation of the Japanese Soldiers. I lined the short stretch of the highway with soldiers hidden among the thick vegetation and out of sight of the motorized Japanese Soldiers. High-powered weapons were interspersed with light armaments. Browning automatic rifles, Enfields, Shotguns, and Revolvers bore the brunt of the attack from the center. Garands and Grenades formed a phalanx against the main Japanese Army force. As added precautionary measures, I posted 25 soldiers on an intersection that connected Maao Sugar Central to the southeast and the town of Bago west, from the crossing that linked Bago town to Maao Sugar Central and Barrio Maao through Crossing Mining. The Soldiers, I posted at the intersection to the Maao Sugar Central, acted as lookouts for the Japanese Army Reinforcements coming from the town of Bago. Emilio and I reviewed our battle plans, and then we opted for the levees with the watercourse behind us; after we had issued explicit orders to the Soldiers who would unleash the initial volley of fires while the rest of the Soldiers attacked the Japanese Army Convoy on cues.

We had set up thorough preparations and laid out plans for battle position when three truckloads of Japanese Soldiers loomed towards us; the vehicles traveled apart each other. When the lead truck cleared nearly off our left flank, we opened fire, while the second convoy ran smack into our center position, and we let loose barrages of rifle fire into the third truck. We let loose the fusillades while the Japanese Soldiers failed a response. They failed retaliation against us who were well entrenched in ambush positions. When the smoke of gun battle cleared, we counted 17 dead Japanese Soldiers while the remaining Japanese Soldiers fled leaving behind their life-less comrades. Reports from our Intelligence network, which was supplied later to us, indicated that 25 more Japanese Soldiers died on the way and 10 Japanese Soldiers were wounded in the ambush encounter. Among the casualties were dead Japanese Civilians who were long-time residents of the Philippines and held captives in the USAFFE stockades; but freed by the Japanese Army, and who led their compatriots in the hunts for Guerrilla Soldiers in Barrio Maao.

We allowed unhampered the Japanese Army patrol entry into Barrio Maao where they hunted, freely and unmolested, and scru-tinized every area where they suspected the Guerrilla Soldiers hid. The absence of the Guerrilla Soldiers deceived the Japanese Sol-diers with a feeling of victory and over-confidence. Bored, tired and complacent, the Japanese Soldiers dozed off during their return trip and when they least expected it; we surprised them with hail of bullets. The Japanese Soldiers proved inept coping up with ambush situations.

It was ironic that the Japanese Army put up, a year later, a Garri-son in Crossing Mining. They confiscated the house of the Lopez family who owned a hacienda in Crossing Mining, and converted the building into a concrete Garrison with gun apertures from the concrete dome. The Japanese Sentinels utilized the tall mango trees as lookout towers. The Guerrilla Soldiers assault mounted against the Japanese Soldiers in the Garrison ended in a disaster when Lt. Magno Valero chose a moonless and rainy night for a Guerrilla Sol-diers attack. The Japanese Army resisted vigorously, retaliated and routed the attackers' assault. Lt. Valero retreated eastward towards the mountains, along the nearby creek; but the Japanese Soldiers massacred the retreating Guerrilla Soldiers and killed Lieutenant. Valero; and as a result the water flowing in the creek was tainted for days with the blood of the slain bodies of Lieutenant. Valero and his Soldiers.

Our initial ambush proved a resounding success and we had the first taste of ambuscade and battle encounter. The victory buoyed our spirits and egged us on for more battle engagements. We drew battle plans and selected viable targets. With respect to the town of Bago; Barrio Cansilayan stood at the northeastern corner of a square, Barrio Sumag at the northwestern, Crossing Mining at the southeastern, and Bago town at the southwestern section of the imaginary square figure. From Barrio Cansilayan, we drove diagonally to Bago town, which was cuddled by Bago River in its southern side, and the Guimaras Strait on the western flank. A National Highway 22 kilometers, north from Bacolod City, parted the town and drove straight into the town plaza at the center of the town and forked; right, to the town Municipal Building and a few meters left, then right a few more meters, another half a kilometer east before the highway extended southward through Bago Bridge after which it branched again; left to Barrio Maao and right to Pulupandan and other towns in southern Negros Islands. The Japanese Army appropriated the Bago town Municipal Building and fortified it into a Garrison, which linked other Japanese Army Garrisons in Bacolod City, Murcia, and Pulupandan; and collectively, these Garrisons were prongs of the Japanese Army Forces aimed into the very heart of the Guerrilla hideouts in the Canlaon Mountains.

Figure 6 illustrated an ambush on 3 truckloads of Japanese Soldiers in transit from raids.

The absence of road linking the town of Bago directly to Barrio Cansilayan worked in our favor because the attacking Japanese Soldiers deprived the use of motor vehicles drew delayed
reinforcements from other Japanese Army Garrisons. The abundance of orchard trees inside the town served well too, our objectives; the vegetation covered our covert movements and hid
us while we took the routes available for our retreat. I posted
25 soldiers at the town entrance from the north and another
25 men at the town exit to the south; the men were fully armed
and they were capable of defending themselves against the Japanese Army reinforcements coming from the north and south.
My main concern was the Japanese Army Garrison, the fortified
Town Municipal Building so I had some of my Soldiers infiltrate
the peripheries of the Japanese Army Garrison, days earlier, with
the mission of gathering useful data such as the strength and
disposition of the Japanese Army inside the Municipal Building.
When the Japanese Army Garrison had been cased, we closed
in on the Japanese Army defenses on midnight of August 10,
1942 and surprised the Japanese Soldiers who were busy at work;
the Japanese Soldiers were loading stacks of rifles into a waiting
truck destined for Bacolod City with the arms shipment. The Japanese Soldiers, with their hands at work, were unarmed when we
swooped down on them. We tied their hands, and bound their
bodies together in groups and herded them to the seashore
where we mowed them down with Browning automatic rifle fires.
Not one of the 15 Japanese Soldiers ever came out alive from
the carnage so we gathered 37 assorted firearms with rounds of
ammunitions, built a bonfire and set the armory to flames. Most
of the weapons came from the sugar cane plantation Owners,
who lived nearby, and who surrendered the firearms, the others
were left behind by the slain Japanese Soldiers who guarded the
Garrison; they all proved unserviceable.

Our triumphs emboldened us and our successes attracted more
manpower into our camp even as we welcome them for I needed
more soldiers in guarding our defenses. The additional support
groups facilitated our intrusions deeper into the Japanese Army

defense lines and persuaded us into the selection of Pulupandan town as the next target for assault. Pulupandan town was 33
kilometers south of Bacolod City to the point where the National Highway parted into a junction leading to the town west of
the National Highway, while the Highway led to other southern
towns of Negros Islands. The junction point was known as Crossing Pulupandan, and was 10 kilometers away to the town proper.
Our raiding teams arrived from Barrio Abuanan through Crossing Mining, down to the road crossing south of Bago town after
the Bago Bridge, and we established battle lines from Crossing
Pulupandan where I posted 50 Soldiers on both sides of the
National Highway as lookouts for the Japanese Army reinforcements coming from the north and south of the highway. I negotiated the distance of 10 kilometers of the two-way Municipal road
that served as entrance and exit between Crossing Pulupandan
and the center of the town. Sitio Katol intersected the road bare-
ly 4 kilometers to the town plaza, and I designated Sitio Katol
as our intermediary assembly point between our targets and the
National Highway, our escape route. We hid our truck in Sitio
Katol, and I posted some of my heavily armed Soldiers for the
protection of our transport vehicle. The rest of the raiding teams
approached the Japanese Army Garrison of Pulupandan town.

The Municipal road from Crossing Pulupandan drove into
the center of the eastern periphery of the town plaza where it
branched north to the town Municipal Building, and south passing by the Japanese Army Garrison before the road turned right
towards the Pulupandan Wharf. The Japanese Army sequestered
the houses owned by the Montilla family and fortified the buildings into a Japanese Army Garrison in the town of Pulupandan.
The Japanese Army Garrison faced the municipal road while the
seashore was at its back.

The Japanese Soldiers stacked sandbags around the buildings,
barricaded the Garrison with pillboxes, and utilized an alley that
separated the two buildings as entrance and exit passage to and
from the Garrison while the fortification was concealed from view
from the town streets by lush growths of trees and thick vegeta-

tion. I availed of the services of my ablest Soldier who penetrated the Japanese Army defense lines by residing, weeks earlier, in the town and observing meticulously the Japanese Soldiers daily activities around the Garrison. He logged faithfully the Japanese Army activities; movements as well as the daily disposition of the Japanese Soldiers and his extensive reporting helped crystallized my strategy for the assault.

Sgt. Emilio Ermio and Sgt. Oscar Custodio who were both US-AFFE Soldiers, another Guerrilla Leader and I divided the town into assault zones. Emilio Ermio's Soldiers watched for any Japanese Army reinforcement coming from Crossing Pulupandan, and attacked the eastern flank of the Japanese Army Garrison. Oscar Custodio assigned a squad of his riflemen southwest of the town plaza, as deterrent against the Japanese Army reinforcement coming from Pulupandan Wharf, which the Japanese Army utilized for berthing their warships, two kilometers from the town plaza to the seashore. Orchard trees and wild vegetation on vacant land that extended to the shoreline bordered the southern side of the Garrison. We deployed five Soldiers behind each vacant store, houses and a gasoline station that faced the Japanese Garrison across the Municipal roads. Sixty-five of our heavily armed Soldiers were positioned from the northern and western sides of the Garrison, who braced for the frontal assault of the Japanese Army Garrison.

I sneaked into the Japanese Army Garrison from the rear while one of my Soldiers and I advanced very slowly because the thick growths of orchard trees hampered our progress. The Japanese Sentinels strung empty bottles with pieces of strings tied to the tree branches of the *senequella*[24] trees; movement among the orchard trees caused collisions among the hanging empty bottles, and the ensuing ripples produced banging and tingling sounds, which alerted the Japanese Soldiers of an intrusion into their defense perimeters. My Soldier and I untied methodically each empty bottle in our efforts at deactivating the Japanese Senti-

24. Philippine tropical fruit.

nels' warning system while we inched our way into the Japanese Army Garrison perimeters. My Soldier and I moved closest to the ground floors of the buildings, and we discovered that the Japanese Guards were half-naked in their under wears and were fast asleep. I tossed grenades after grenades into the laps of the unconscious Japanese Guards, and the loud explosions signaled the commencement of the Guerrilla Soldiers assault of the Japanese Army Garrison. We concentrated our firepower towards the buildings while other Japanese Soldiers awakened and leaped into all directions but our barrages pinned them down to death.

Awakened by intense gun fires and loud explosions, the town people fled to seashores and riverbanks when the Japanese Army Contingents who guarded the Pulupandan Wharf retaliated with bombardments of their cannons. I felt that it was time for disengagement, so I fired retreat signals and all of us raced back to Sitio Katol, the designated reassembly point, and where our transport truck was waiting. We tarried for awhile while we waited for the rest of the soldiers; then I realized that the riflemen who guarded the west flank against the Japanese Army possible reinforcements coming from the Wharf were missing. We motored to another pre-designated reassembly point, which was beside the mango tree that thrived a few meters away from the foot of Bago Bridge and along the road towards Crossing Mining. We waited for another hour; still there was no sign of the missing Squad. We left finally for our hideouts in Barrio Abuanan thinking that the missing Soldiers were killed until the next day when I was informed that the Riflemen took a different route during the retreat. The Guerrilla Soldiers raid into the Japanese Army Garrison in the town of Pulupandan in the middle of the night of September 9, 1942 netted us a hefty score; 82 Japanese Soldiers were killed and a Filipino puppet Policeman of the Japanese Army died.

Barrio Sumag was 10 kilometers south of Bacolod City, with an entrance bridge from the City, a market place and school buildings at a junction between the National Highway to Negros Islands' southern towns and a road leading 10 kilometers east

to Barrio Abuanan. We approached the Barrio in disguised at-
tires of varied hue; we were dressed in farmers' garb, some of us
wore handkerchiefs wound around our heads as we walked on
rice land dikes and pretended that we were farmers marching
to work. We took ambush positions and set up a trap at a cemetery a kilometer south of Barrio Sumag school buildings site. I
deployed my Soldiers in ditches along the National Highway and
waited for the arrival of our prey, which appeared in a short time
and rushed headlong into our entrapment. I signaled the truck
driver into full stop and the driver slammed his vehicular brakes
to a screeching halt. When I approached the truck, the lone pas-
senger was surprised at seeing me again, because months earlier,
I commandeered vehicles in the name of the USAFFE and Fritz
Von Couphman, the Manager of the La Carlota Sugar Central
had the unpleasant task of surrendering to me the property
which the USAFFE needed. At this time, I offered Couphman
a choice; the truck he was riding on or his life and Couphman
readily gave up the truck so I let the driver look for transportation and Von Couphman and his driver completed their trip
to Bacolod City. On October 5, 1942, I acquired a Loadmaster
truck loaded with 250 cans of kerosene without firing a single
shot. We used the truck in transporting rice grains from Barrio
Cansilayan to Barrio Pandanon for the supply of the Divisional
Headquarters of the Negros Islands Resistance Movement; and
the kerosene substituted for electricity, which provided lighting
for houses built beside the hills.

The Japanese Imperial Army displayed its armed might when
16 truck loads of Japanese Soldiers raided Barrio Maao while we
waited for their return at Hacienda Rufina, a sugar cane plantation located nearer east to Crossing Mining than west to the town
of Bago. The farmland was patches of two sugar cane plantation
with a Lane that separated them running from the National
Highway towards Bago River banks. Emilio Ermio and I mapped
out an ambush strategy; Ermio's forces would compose the assaulting group against the Japanese Army convoy coming back
east from Barrio Maao while my forces lined the stretch of the

National Highway that extended down to the Lane, which intercepted the National Highway at Hacienda Rufina. Emilio Ermio and I agreed that Emilio's Soldiers attacked the five remaining trucks as soon as the 11 trucks of the Japanese Army Soldiers cleared his position. The whole idea was weaning the last five trucks away from the 11 Japanese Army convoy and together, our forces attacked and decimated the remaining five truckloads of Japanese Soldiers.

Figure 7 demonstrated a successful ambush of 16 truckloads of Japanese Soldiers and the capture alive of 21 Japanese Soldiers after the battle encounter.

Emilio Ermio played a cruel joke on me when his group of Soldiers attacked the Japanese Army convoy after the first five trucks cleared his positions; his action proved to be the exact opposite of our agreed plan of attack. The Japanese Forces from

the remaining 11 trucks leaped from their vehicles, swarmed towards us, sprayed us madly with bullets and fought furiously like
irate hornets from embattled beehives. The sugar cane leaves
rustled like corn popping with the rain of bullets, and the canes
cracked, ripped or tore away from the impact of the Japanese
Army fusillades. Adding insult to my injured feelings due to the
unexpected change in our battle plan, Emilio Ermio withdrew,
after a few minutes of firefights; and his forces withdrew also
from the battle scene leaving me in contention against the Japanese Army aggressive Soldiers. Prone on furrows, ducked in
ditches and under the cover of the verdant sugar cane growths,
my Soldiers and I dished out to the Japanese Forces the firepower that we possessed; Browning automatic rifles, Garands,
Enfields, Shotguns, revolvers, and grenades went into action.
The Japanese Soldiers, sensing Emilio Ermio's forces retreat,
were emboldened in their counter attack that, over confident,
they stood upright in their pursuit. We found very effective the
Shotguns in ripping wide open the Japanese Soldiers' stomachs;
while the Japanese Soldiers surged forward with their own plan
of encircling my forces against the riverbanks nearby. The armored car broke away from the Japanese Army column and
spearheaded the Japanese pincer drive against us. My Rifleman
knocked out of commission the Japanese armored vehicle with
his Browning automatic gun and armored-piercing bullets; but
the Japanese Soldiers executed their encirclement plan. I was at
the west wing of the sugar cane plantation left of the Lane, and I
took cover under the sugar canes and behind the clumps of bamboo trees growing along the highway; while the Japanese Forces
concentrated on the sugar cane plantation east of the Lane. The
lush sugar canes standing eight feet tall entangled with mesh of
the cane-dried leaves provided me a screen from the advancing
enemy troops so the Japanese Soldiers overlooked my presence
when they advanced from the highway to the riverbank along
the Lane. I kept on shooting at the Japanese Soldiers, with my
Shooting Master, while they passed by me, intent on enveloping my forces against the riverbank. I followed the Japanese

Soldiers who were in a column and I shot them from behind their backs until the Japanese Forces were hemmed in by the luxuriant, reedy and tall grasses thriving along the riverbanks and the lush sugar canes growing on both sides of the Lane. My Soldiers turned around from the National Highway towards the Bago River banks while they were kept hidden from view from the Japanese Soldiers by the equally luxuriant growing sugar canes as they closed in on the trapped Japanese Soldiers. My Soldiers and I had the option of either killing the trapped Japanese Soldiers; however, the Japanese Soldiers started throwing away their rifles and they raised their hands as indication of surrender. We disarmed the Japanese Soldiers, tied their hands behind their backs (the Japanese way), marched them across the bridge that spanned Bago River, herded them down the Bago River banks under Quezon Bridge, and lodged them in the prison caves which I devised beneath the hedge grows along the Bago River banks.

I had a sub command post, 250 feet away from the prison caves where I hid the Japanese prisoners, readied for reassembly after the ambush, where women prepared food for tired and hungry ambushers, and prayed for the success of the battle outcome. Young and beauteous ladies heaped praises on me for the successful results of the ambuscade to the consternation of Emilio Ermio and his "disappearing soldiers" who withdrew prematurely from the battlefields. On October 30, 1942, in the fierce battle at Hacienda Rufina of the town of Bago, my Guerrilla Band accounted for the killing of 87 Japanese Soldiers on the spot, 19 more Japanese Soldiers died later, and 21 Japanese Soldiers were captured alive.

News of the battle encounter at Hacienda Rufina spread like wildfires and reached the knowledge of Col. Ernesto Mata, Division Commander, Northern Negros Sector of the Negros Islands Resistance Movement, who summoned me to his mountain Headquarters. Profusely gratified and effusively appreciative of my achievement, he promoted me, on the spot, to the rank of First Lieutenant; moreover, he came down with me and accompanied me to my hideout wanting the inspection of the captive Japanese Soldiers; unfortunately, we found all the Japanese prisoners dead.

My soldiers, during my absence, poked fun of the Japanese prisoners; they tied one hand of each Japanese captive behind his back, and armed the free hand with dried sugarcane for a truncheon. Under the pretenses of learning martial arts, they badgered the hapless Japanese prisoners into teaching those lessons, while the Guerrilla Soldier opponents were armed with bolos, which they utilized in slashing the Japanese Soldiers, resulting into a one-sided and merciless hacking of the Japanese captives to death. My Soldiers slaughtered the Japanese Soldiers, broiled and ate the Japanese Soldiers' livers, which they claimed to be the cleanest of all the animals' entrails; in an only instance when I lost complete control of my Soldiers.

The Japanese Forces contrived all means of snaring the Guerrilla Soldiers in suspected places and on a market day in Barrio Sumag, the Japanese Army hid their vehicles near the bridge, walked across, and the Japanese Soldiers caught the market people in surprise; they rounded up all the males, tied their hands behind their backs and loaded them into their vans. I decided an attack so my Soldiers and I moved cautiously towards the school buildings on an adjacent lot to the market place where I signaled for the commencement of the attack; I cued my Bugler into sounding the battle charge on an improvised battle hymn. The Bugler played the battle notes that might have stumped the Japanese Soldiers more than stupefied them with the non-descript and bizarre notes of the martial tunes. Recovering from their senses, the Japanese Soldiers faced my Soldiers across the Barrio road that separated the market place from the school lot, and with blazing guns, the Japanese Soldiers emerged from empty market stalls in a furious assault against us, thereby giving the Filipino captives chances of escape, who seized the opportunity of unguarded moment, and who bolted the Japanese Army van, dived into and swan across Sumag River to safety. Other Guerrilla Soldiers who patronized the market place and who were unaware of my battle tactics scampered towards the riverbanks. The Japanese Soldiers and the Guerrilla Soldiers locked into combat, until the Japanese Army reinforcements arrived and I ordered a retreat. A running battle ensued; the Guerrilla Soldiers withdrew while the Japanese Soldiers ran in hot pursuit of us, so I stopped, but I stopped at every 30-yard distance that I yielded to the Japanese Army even as I assessed the situation. Whenever the Japanese Soldiers neared us, we offered stiff resistance; thus delaying their swift advances until we ceded another piece of ground. My Guerrilla Soldiers beat a diagonal withdrawal from Barrio Sumag to Barrio Abuanan along the road that linked Barrio Sumag to Barrio Abuanan while the Japanese Soldiers pressed on their attacks against us, so my Soldiers worked feverishly on the demolition of the wooden bridge along the way. I held the pursuing Japanese Soldiers at bay, dishing out fair exchanges for the bullets they rained on us; and if there was a time when I felt I was closest to death, the time came when the Japanese Soldiers' bullets whizzed past all over my body at a hair's breathe. Strange as it might seem, it was one of my Soldiers at my back who caught a bullet through his waist, but he, too, survived. Another of my Soldiers incurred a grazing wound at his right shoulder, but I lost another loyal Soldier. We killed 35 Japanese Soldiers during our encounter with the Japanese Army in Sumag on November 17, 1942, and we could have inflicted more casualties on them, had they followed us while we retreated to Barrio Abuanan. When the bridge collapsed after we had crossed it, we taunted the Japanese Soldiers into coming after us and capturing us, but the Japanese Soldiers stopped their pursuit and withdrew too. We planned on reestablishing another battle positions once we had crossed the bridge of the Balulan Creek and demolished it, and launched hand grenades assault when the Japanese Soldiers were crossing the Creek.

The Japanese Army did not take our depredations lying down; the Japanese Patrols hounded us, so we waited for them at Sitio

Ubay, a small community at Crossing Bago. We chose the sugar cane plantation where the canes were growing tall, and the canals around the plantation were blanketed with tall and thick reeds and grasses. I hid my armed Soldiers among the verdant greeneries before three truckloads of Japanese Soldiers coming from the south, loomed before us. The trucks negotiated the road that curved to the right towards us and supposedly turned left into the entrance of Bago Bridge from the south. We loosed barrages of our firepower on the last two vehicles just when the trucks negotiated the curb towards us, forcing the trucks into a zigzag stop just before the bridge where the bodies of the dead 15 Japanese Soldiers were dumped. One of my Soldiers was overwhelmed with elation over the fleeing Japanese Soldiers that he threw caution to the winds, ran in pursuit of the Japanese Soldiers with barking guns from his hip; but the remaining retreating Japanese Soldiers retaliated causing the death of another of my brave Soldier.

Early the following year, the Japanese Army was in hot pursuit of my Guerrilla Soldiers, so I sauntered eastward; we moved from my mountain hideout in Barrio Bacong, crossed the Pula River and hiked over the Tabucol mountain range. We were in the plateau after the hills and on National Highway two kilometers away from the nearest hill. The Japanese Army utilized the National Highway in their commute between Mambucal from the east to Bacolod City to the west. My Soldiers and I staged another ambush while we concealed ourselves in ditches along the highway, hiding our presence under the overlay of shrubs and wild tall grasses that grew on top of the banks of the water canals. A truckload of Japanese Soldiers coming from Mambucal wheeled, as we had anticipated, into our concealments, and before the Japanese Soldiers sensed the entrapments, we heaped bullets and grenades on the Japanese Convoy; and when the smoke cleared we counted 15 dead Japanese Soldiers. Our ambush and victory on January 16, 1943 at Barrio San Miguel, was our belated way of celebrating the New Year's Day.

The ambuscades were our direct confrontation with the Japanese Army; but I realized that we needed a base of operation and our Guerrilla Band needed logistics and communication system for the prosecution of a sustained resistance against the Japanese Forces and for a build-up of our morale.

CHAPTER 6

Bivouac

The havoc that we wrought on the Japanese Army drew the indignation of our enemies; so the Japanese Expeditionary Forces probed deeper into our locations. Our position was untenable because the Barrio populations were apt for hostages, which the Japanese Army held in exchange for our surrender, so we distanced ourselves from Barrio Cansilayan and Barrio Abuanan and swam across Bago River to the mountain foothills.

What were once the tranquil mountainsides of Negros Islands transformed into the refugees' havens and the guerrilla fighters' communes. The wide divide of the waterway and the steep banks of Bago River drew an unofficial demarcation line between the Japanese Army occupied war zone and the Guerrilla Fighters free zone. From the far northeast source of Bago River at Barrio Igmayaan, came next in line of succession down the river, Barrio Komalisquis where the Negros Islands Resistance Movement established its Divisional Headquarters. Barrio Komalisquis was serrated with hundreds of ravines, creeks, ridges, streams, gorges and mounts that the Division Headquarters was seemingly out of reach of the Japanese Army's hands. Upward from Barrio Komalisquis to Canlaon Mountains was Sitio Bidio dubbed by the Guerrilla Soldiers as the "lion's den" because it was the hideout of Col. Ernesto Mata, the Deputy Commander of Negros Islands Resistance Movement and undoubtedly the lion of Canlaon Mountains, battle-wise. The lion's den connoted a lair for the training of lion cubs; Sitio Bidio was a place where errant soldiers were recalled to the Headquarters for retraining, reassignment, reprimand or for detention, but the best from the packs of soldiers were promoted by the Deputy Division Commander who lived in the nearby, "Lion's Den."

Major Ernesto Mata was the young Battalion Commander who guarded the Banago Wharf in Bacolod City when the Japanese Forces landed on May 22, 1942, and he was one of the United States Armed Forces in the Far East (USAFFE) Soldiers who did not surrender to the Japanese Army. He fled immediately to the Canlaon Mountains so that he was never imprisoned by the Japanese Army unlike many others who were incarcerated by the Japanese Army until they escaped from the Japanese Army captivity. Major Mata roamed the mountains until he entertained the thought of leaving Negros Islands for Luzon Island; and he was on his way on a horse back leaving the mountains when one of the followers of Mayor Alfredo Montelibano, Sr. of Bacolod City encountered Major Mata and the messenger informed Major Mata of the desire of Mayor Montelibano for a meeting. The meeting resulted into the organization of the Free Negros Islands Government led by Military Governor Alfredo Montelibano, Sr. and the Negros Islands Resistance Movement led by Colonel Ernesto Mata as Deputy Islands Commander and Division Commander of Northern Sector of Negros Islands.

We were at the initial stage of Guerrilla Resistance to the Japanese Army; and many of the USAFFE Soldiers who did not surrender to the Japanese Army opted for the mountains for refuge. We established military territory by claiming a portion of the mountains that best suited us for hiding, whereas the Japanese Army in Bacolod City imprisoned many of the USAFFE Soldiers who surrendered. Many escaped from the Japanese Army stockade and headed for the mountains but they encountered complications when the USAFFE Soldiers who did not surrender suspected them as Japanese Army collaborators; many of them were interrogated, imprisoned and some were executed to death by the zealous USAFFE Soldiers who had already established territories in the mountains.

Suspicions reigned even among the USAFFE Soldiers who did not surrender to the Japanese Army but opted for the mountains. There were doubts as to the motivations and the loyalty of each other. Some of the USAFFE Officers who negotiated the surrender with the Japanese Army were slain by those who resisted surrender. There was a question of leadership, which each other's claimed should be based upon each other's standards. There were questions of territorial jurisdictions among the sets of the budding Guerrilla Resistance Movement organizers. Many of the controversies were settled in killings of valuable emerging leaders of the Guerrilla movement; others were betrayed to the Japanese Army who likewise executed them to death.

The reorganization of Negros Islands Resistance Movement was completed later after contact was established with the United States Liberation Forces. Division, Regiment, Battalion, and Company down to the smallest military unit were reconstituted and filled up with military officers and personnel. The Philippine Army that fought side by side with the United States Liberation Forces, against the Japanese Forces, was the amalgamation of all the Guerrilla Bands of Soldiers or Guerrilla Groups of Soldiers who resisted the Japanese Army.

Below Sitio Bidio, Nature carved a gorge from the Canlaon Mountains, and made it into Spa, Negros Islanders called it the Mambucal Spring Summer Resort. Barrio San Miguel, on the other hand, interposed the National Highway between the Mambucal Spring Summer Resort and the Bago Ferry Mambucal Bridge; and the Barrio harbored Pula River, on its southern perimeter, that flowed almost parallel with the National Highway down to the western length of Bago River at Sitio Cabagsiwan. Pula River streamed from Mambucal Spring Summer Resort in the northeast side of Canlaon Mountains and cascaded northeast down along a mountain range until it formed a delta with Bago River at Sitio Cabagsiwan. The delta at Sitio Cabag-

siwan was the initial seat of government of Free Bago when the
Japanese Army landed in Negros Islands, until it transferred
deeper into the Canlaon Mountains. I designated the mountain range running along Pula River as the northern flank of
my circumferential Defense Line. Protected by the 500-foot
mountain range and the Pula River in the north from the intrusion of the Japanese Army, I settled at the delta of Sitio
Cabagsiwan, my vanguard at the north against the Japanese
Army threat coming from the National Highway between Murcia in the west to Mambucal in the east. The precipitous banks
of the river and the deep water of Bago River at my right side
obviated the Japanese Army forces into my position while the
shallow and widest expanse of the river in front, forestalled the
Japanese Army frontal encroachment, and the sharply sloping
riverbanks and the high hills shielded Sitio Cabagsiwan; but I
bypassed it because Sitio Cabagsiwan lacked an overview of the
Japanese Army approaches from the distance. Sitio Buri came
as the next rampart along my Defense Line; it was weaned into
the Guerrilla Soldiers side of the free zone from the Japanese
Army war zone across the river, by Bago River; while Sitio Buri
was a patch of farm land which served our purpose for food
supply, and the place served as rest and recreation center and
an important land mark in our crammed defensive position.
The succeeding important points as we glided down and along
the water's edge were Sitio Sanduñgaw in the Guerrilla zone
in tandem with Sitio Udag across the river in the Japanese
zone. Sitio Udag was located on top of the riverbank, which
had a passage, a hollowed slope from the riverbank, for travelers down the river. I utilized Sitio Udag as my subcommand
post for transmission of messages between the Japanese zone
and the Guerrilla zone, and for foraging and combat operations into the Japanese zone. Messengers were housed in Sitio
Udag as well as the horses, which they used for speedy transportation back and forth. Trespassers were interrogated and
screened at this point, before they were allowed down the river while Sentries hidden behind boulders watched their every

step. Strangers were rarely allowed access to Sitio Sanduñgaw
because this other subcommand post played the most vital
role in my intelligence network. Sitio Sanduñgaw was a basin
of a stream that oozed into Bago River and harbored wild flo-
ra, tall bamboo trees, and thick thorny thickets. I built make-
shift huts under the canopy of thick verdures, and provided
potable water, piped in by lengths of bamboo poles that si-
phoned tap water from a spring up the bank of the stream and
down to our huts. Sitio Sanduñgaw was well guarded because
this subcommand post was another rest and recreation center
of my Soldiers and above all other considerations, our telephone communications was based in this place. I had secured
a telephone set, one of those utilized by sugar cane plantation
owners in their communication with the sugar centrals or with
other nearby land owners and I set up the telephone wires on
branches of trees growing along the banks of the stream up
to my Headquarters; so men who disguised themselves as fire-
wood gatherers doubled as caretakers and guards, protected
our communication equipments.

Sitio Tanag stood across the river and formed part of the periphery of Barrio Cansilayan but the place was equally important because it provided a passageway through the river and
linked Barrio Cansilayan to the Guerrilla zone at its counterpart, Sitio Dagasanan, so called because the water current at
Sitio Dagasanan was so strong for swimming against. I posted
Guerrilla Sentinels as watchdogs against the entry of the Japanese Forces through these points. Sitio Inambacan, a southern river passage that connected our zone into a farmland
between Barrio Abuanan and Barrio Antipuluan; was a place
that played vital role in the procurement of food supply from
the harvest of the farmlands. Barrio Capilian was the last fron-
tier in our southern Defense Line, which extended to as far as
Barrio Antipuluan and the Hinaluan River. Sitio Capilian and
Sitio Inambacan had their counterpart in the Guerrilla Zone
in Sitio Cabcab, which was well guarded by my Soldiers as well.

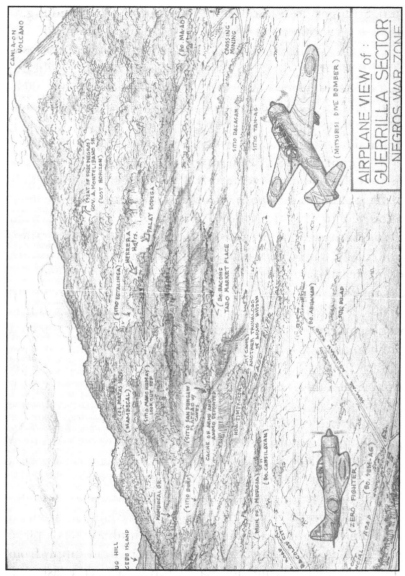

Figure 8 divided Negros Islands between the Guerrilla Soldiers Free Zone and the Japanese Army War Zone.

With the commencement of my Defense Line from Sitio Cabagsiwan, northeast of the Bago River down to Sitio Buri, Sitio Sanduñgaw, Sitio Dagasanan, and Sitio Cabcab southwest in front of me, I was inside a horse-shoe shaped defensive perimeters with

Sitio Maghumay located at a higher elevation at my back while the Canlaon Mountains loomed farthest. Bago River was a long and winding river that flowed from the mountains in the east to the sea in the west; it was never navigable both ways along its course, except for the river crossings at Bago Ferry Mambucal Bridge in the east, the railroad bridge of Quezon Bridge at Crossing Mining, and the Bago Bridge linking Bacolod City to the southern towns through the town of Bago. The long and winding Bago River had a series of strong current accentuated by the presence of boulders and underwater slippery stones, which made river crossings very difficult. The occasional deep body of water interspersed; but the Japanese Soldiers crossing the river on *bancas*[24] became virtually sitting ducks for sniper attacks hidden on riverbanks from the sides of the Guerrilla Zone. I extended west the tentacles of my Defense Line to as far as Sitio Kipot a third of a kilometer from the Sumag Bridge and a hearing distance of the Japanese Army Patrol who passed by the bridge. Sitio Balulan followed Sitio Kipot in parallel with the river linking the Barrio Cansilayan River Bridge and the Sumag River Bridge along with the road linking Barrio Sumag through the Sumag-Abuanan road crossing to Barrio Abuanan and Barrio Cansilayan. I designated Sitio Dulao as my Advance Command Post after Sitio Balulan because Sitio Dulao was in an intermediate distance between Barrio Abuanan and Barrio Sumag while Sitio Bulad followed in the order of the Defense Line; however, all these defense points ended in my Command Post at Barrio Bacong.

Barrio Bacong, a political subdivision of the Municipality of Bago, was a hilltop overlooking Bago River and had a commanding view of the sites along and across the river that encompassed my Defense Line. The sites across the river were a hearing distance from Barrio Bacong while travelers on both sides of the river were visible from the hilltop with the use of the binoculars. I was in possession of a field-type set of binoculars, which I contracted and retracted, depending upon the size and distance of the object I wanted mag-

---

24. Boats hollowed out of logs and fitted with bamboo pole outriggers.

nified. This indispensable pair of field binoculars enabled us the
detection and the monitor of the Japanese Soldiers movements at
far distances before the Japanese Army penetrated our Defense
Line. Barrio Bacong was accessible to the lowlanders from the west
and even residents of Bacolod City and nearby towns, those who
offered merchandise for sale; and from people coming from Canlaon town in the east coming over the hills of the mountain range
that parted Negros Oriental from Negros Occidental, for purposes of trade and commerce, because Barrio Bacong emerged as the
biggest market place outside of the Japanese Army-held territories.
I channeled whatever financial supports I received from patriotic
benefactors into the hands of the hundreds of stallholders in the
market in recognition of the market people loyalty and support
to my Guerrilla organization. The Free Negros Islands Government levied taxes on the businesses in Barrio Bacong, and the rev-
enues from Barrio Bacong contributed immensely to the coffers
of the Free Negros Islands Government Treasury. The Japanese
Soldiers, ironically, patronized the market on Sundays by coming
to the market place through the Bago River Bridge and to Barrio
Maao where they left their vehicles and went on foot, unmolested
by the Guerrilla Soldiers, to Barrio Bacong. The Japanese Army
discovered the thriving business in Barrio Bacong, and on several
occasions, became attracted to the beautiful Filipino venders so
that the Japanese Soldiers presented themselves as buyers. The
trading transactions were sham, but the Japanese Soldiers never
realized that the Guerrilla Soldiers were the sources of funds for
the business activities in the market. The market people who were
beneficiaries of the Guerrilla Soldiers funding were Guerrilla Soldiers informers on the Japanese Soldiers movements; and these
beneficiaries of the capitalization from the Guerrilla Soldiers con-
stituted the 500-strong civilian armed supporters who hid their
weapons, either firearms or bolos, in the thick greeneries nearby
for easy access in case of exigency.

Standing on the hilltop of Barrio Bacong, and facing the east
direction in front of him, a spectator's search for tableland ended in vain, for only patches of verdures clambering up the moun-

tain walls greeted his gaze. The Japanese Patrol took the southern approaches from Barrio Maao, the rugged hills of Sitio Mahilum, and passed by Barrio Bacong, on their way to the highly elevated Manghumay (1,022 feet above sea level), overhead, but they always missed Sitio Egtalinga (1,000 feet above sea level) below. Sitio Egtalinga was a stone's throw from Barrio Bacong Tabô market, so close that the footsteps of passersby through the market were within earshot's hearing distance (25 feet) from Sitio Egtalinga; still I designated Sitio Egtalinga as my Rear Command Post and my Headquarters. Patriotic and loyal Filipino Civilians who were familiar with Barrio Bacong topography brought me to the place where we hacked secret passages under the canopies of densely tangled and thorny tree vines. Mother Nature grafted 3,000 square meters of land, embedded the lot to the mountain walls and cloistered the real estate under the thick and luxuriant forest trees and shrubbery; and then, Mother Nature assembled three big rocks into a triangle and endowed the center space with flowing fresh potable spring water, as Nature's crowning glory to its work of arts. We constructed water turbine and harnessed the rapids flowing from the spring, and generated electricity for lightning; but most importantly for the electric power of our radio receiving sets. We installed telephone lines and linked Sitio Sanduñgaw to Sitio Egtalinga; as a result, we completed our telephone communication system. We made clearings and built living quarters under the forest trees beside the mountain walls; thus, we converted Sitio Egtalinga as our Rear Command Post and Headquarters for military and social functions.

We held dances whenever the occasions warranted; and we tuned in to the Voice of America radio broadcasts for music or we strummed the strings of our guitars for local tunes. The lyrics of our favorite song appealed to both patriotism and reality:

> From up the mountains
> We view the lowlands
> Those lovely rolling plains
> Which God has given us

Thus sadly staring
Our hearts are aching
Waiting and wishing for
Those dark days to pass
We are not brigands
We are not bandits
We are just men
Desirous to be free
For though we suffer
And though we perish
Sweeter to us is
Death than Slavery
If the hills could tell a story
They would speak of our privation
How we struggled with starvations
On those lonely mountain sides
How with scanty arms and weapons
We defied the naughty Nippon
How we groaned in cold and sickness
Everything to us denied
Yet we laugh at all those hardships
We can sing away our troubles
We will carry on the struggle
Though we perish in the strife
For we've decided
And we're united
To fight for freedom
As our way of life

Melody was adapted from "Wine and Music".
P. Velasquez and C. Hofileña composed the lyrics.

We were in the first step of flight of stairs to the highest peak
of Canlaon Mountains; and we already felt the rigors of a journey
on foot from Bacolod City over 30 kilometers of unpaved roads,
unbeaten trails, round-about routes, stony courses, and laborious

ascent up the hills, which discouraged us from shuttling between the City and the Bivouac. My mind dwelt on the thousands of the population who were used to the comforts of city living, but who were forced at crossing rivers and scaling the mountains in their escape from the reach of the fearsome Japanese Army. We all suffered from insufficiency of shelter, food, medicine and even clothing; for we were all left to Nature in fending for ourselves.

Several young ladies in my Bivouac came from decent families in Bacolod City and towns; the Benitez sisters from Bacolod City, the Makilan sisters from Murcia, and Gloria Gubaton from the same town, were some of those who chose the hardships in the mountains over the comforts of the city. They were some of the women who were in their prime of youth who should have been in schools or in the practice of their professions; but who got mixed up with war and forced into spending their lives in the jungle for we all knew that a step inside the Japanese Army-held territory might end up in capture, torture or even death.

We kept tuned to the broadcasts from the Voice of America and the news of the Allied Power's victories in land, in sea and in the sky kept our morale high; and we knew that every time the Allied Powers gained ground, the liberation of the Philippines was drawing nearer. The fear of the Japanese Army, notwithstanding, and the hardships we endured, we looked forward to the day of the end of the war while we took comfort in another favorite and morale-boosting song.

> You told us to surrender
> You sons of the rising sun
> As if we have no honor
> Nor will to fire a gun
> You threaten us with murder
> And frighten us with lies
> Saying you're the master
> Of land and seas and skies
> Bomb every town and border
> Shell every house and farm

But we will not surrender
Though blood flows from our arms
We will carry on the struggle
Though we perish in the strife
Fighting always for freedom
On land and seas and skies
There is freedom in the mountainsides
There is music in the hills
Why should we give up liberty?
For gloomy doubtful fate
We won't believe another word
From sons of treachery
But we will carry on the fight
 Onward to victory!

P. Velasquez and C. Hofileña composed the lyrics
while B. Paculan composed the tune.

We entertained guests in my Bivouac, and my Rear Command
Post buzzed with preparations for a visit of a very special Guest; as
we covered the estate with matting and the women took charge
of the beautification and cleanliness, in anticipation of the arrival of Colonel Ernesto Mata and his Party on an inspection tour.
I took this visit as a rare opportunity for my Soldiers of meeting,
in person, the Deputy Commander of the Negros Islands Resistance Movement, and I set aside protocols by seating the Privates
alternately with Officers; thus exposing my Soldiers to vantage
points around the conference table. Colonel Ernesto Mata expressed satisfaction over the orderliness, cleanliness, and beautification of our camp that he adjudged our Bivouac as the best in
Negros Islands. He thanked me for the food we prepared for his
Party as well as for the sumptuous meals we had served. Turning
his head towards me, after the lunch, he inquired if he could
have my radio receiving sets. It seemed that I could never refuse
the request of the good Colonel, so I parted with my prized possession and gave away the only radio receiving sets that I had, to

him; although I succeeded later in its replacement with brand new sets of radio receiver. When Colonel Mata took liking to my Diary Book, I supplied him with another one, which I procured from the Lopue's Department Store in Bacolod City; and I obtained for him also his favorite brand of cigarettes, in record time, through my undercover agents because we had communication, and transportation systems that complimented our Rear Command Post.

I settled down to the brass tacks of comprehending the exigencies of the myriad problems of inhabitants from Sitio Kipot to our Rear Command Post in Sitio Egtalinga as the problems cropped up. Evacuees reported losses of work animals while others recounted the cruelty of other guerrilla soldiers; so I redressed as fairly as I could, the grievances of the civilian population. I warned with stern admonitions the offenders of minor infraction while the recidivists were penalized with the felons hanged upside down, their feet were securely tied to tree branches, and they were left hanging for hours in the same position, until the aggrieved parties took compassion and pleaded for their release. Twenty thieves were punished that way; and when released, they left the scene of their thievery without ever coming back.

A young man approached me and volunteered his services in support of my Guerrilla Soldiers; so I processed his application for membership until two days later when he came back for an interview. A security check of his background among his neighbors in Barrio Abuanan disclosed that he had committed a crime against chastity, and his admission of similar crimes in the past led to his execution to death for preventing him from joining the Japanese Army.

I was in my Bivouac in Sitio Egtalinga when Felipe Makilan apprised me of the predicament that Manuel Bumaat faced; he was at the brink of death, and Makilan was helpless in averting the tragedy, although he had compassion for the victim. Manuel Bumaat was a hard-working old man who acquired a farmland in Sitio Hagnaya through the dint of hard work. He raised crops, swine, cattle, and poultry, which he shared with the Guerrilla Soldiers and he had lost the life of his son who died fighting in the battlefield of Bataan for the cause of freedom.

The Brigands wanted not only a share of Manuel Bumaat's products, but the Wild Bunch demanded his surrender of his daughters to them. Manuel Bumaat refused at the unreasonable and undignified demands of the brigands and the marauders retaliated by capturing Manuel Bumaat and ordering him into digging his own grave while his captors jeered at him.

"Can you act swiftly and snatch Manuel Bumaat from death?" Felipe pleaded to me.

I gathered a group of my Soldiers and we hurried to Sitio Kipot where we surrounded the marauding band and I ordered the culprits into the release of Manuel Bumaat to which they complied and they freed Manuel Bumaat who was still shaking in his boots while he was coming out of the pit.

"Jorge," commented Manuel Bumaat after his release, "I felt like I was nearing death at every tick of the clock as I dug my own grave."

I advised Manuel Bumaat into transferring his family to Barrio Cansilayan, far from the farmland, for I was certain that the Brigands would never relent from their evil designs.

Many of my Soldiers left my Bivouac; Franco Villafranca left for Panay Island, Fabian Nelda never relished my method of meting out punishments so he left me for good, and Antonio Aurelio told me right before my face that he wanted no part in my battle tactics. He wanted that the Japanese Army attacked us first; instead of the Guerrilla Soldiers tracking down and assaulting the Japanese Soldiers, so he left me, but many others took over their places and the Guerrilla resistance against the Japanese Army went on.

CHAPTER 7

Civilian Supporters

The ravages of war struck horrors, instilled fears and heaped destructions on human lives; and next to bullets, starvation emerged as the most destructive of all the Grim Reapers. Imaginary lines were drawn that spelled the difference between life and death, for the Filipino Civilians were limited to choices of asylum that compromised between survival or death from hunger and bullets. Veiled lines parted Negros Islands into a Japanese Army Zone, the Guerrilla Zone, and the gray line zone of the Filipino Civilians. The cities and the towns belonged to the Japanese Army zone which possessed the sea, air and land transports; hence the industry and commerce belonged to them while the Filipino Civilians who ventured life under Japanese Army control carried on the Japanese Army economy. The Filipino Civilians were hired by the Japanese Army as deck hands in the Japanese fishing boats that trawled the Negros Islands seas; many of them perished by being thrown overboard for crimes of mere ignorance, laziness or flippancy because the Japanese were strict employers who had zero tolerance for mediocrity. The Filipino Civilians were the manufacturers of household items and food products out of scanty materials and they were merchants and traders who utilized transportation that were escorted by the Japanese Soldiers in discouraging ambushes by the Guerrilla Soldiers until the risks of ambuscades far outweighed the profits and business stopped. The ease and comfort of urban life accrued to the benefits of metropolis dwellers but the incessant suspicions and surveillances of the Japanese Army posed constant threats of arrests, brutalities, and even execution to death, depending upon the temperament of the Japanese Soldiers, and the Japanese Army was a taciturn master. The Japanese Army evened the score of the lives of their Soldiers that were lost to ambushes with the lives of the Filipino Civilians who they suspected as perpetrators or who were in connivance with the Guerrilla Soldiers. The Guerrilla Soldiers pounced at every opportunity on the City dwellers with the belief that the urbanites were Japanese Army sympathizers; and therefore, they were traitors who deserved death as punishment.

The Filipino Civilians, living in the gray zone, carried on agriculture. The Filipino Civilians were aged men and women, the widows, the orphans, and the invalids who tilled the outlying farms of the towns; the Japanese Army consider them impotent in waging war against them, and the Japanese Patrols sidetracked them, nevertheless, war never relented on them. The ordeals of Damaso Calansiñgin and Juliana Lumacang, his wife, typified life in the gray area – the zone where both the Japanese Army and the Filipino Guerrilla Soldiers allowed the Filipino Civilians in carrying on with their daily activities; but both the Japanese Army and Guerrilla Soldiers suspected them of aiding one against the other. The couple had more than their share of loyalty to the Country, because they lost a son who fought in the battlefields of Bataan, was among those whom the Japanese Army marched in that infamous Death March from Bataan to the next province of Tarlac where the prisoners were imprisoned in the Japanese Army concentration camp; and where the couple's son died of starvation and sickness. The old couple built their house on an elevated portion of the sugar cane fields at the boundary of Hacienda Puyas and Hacienda San Enrique, about a couple of kilometers southwest of the town of Murcia; the bottom line of choosing the vantage location was the exposure of the house and its surroundings open to the Japanese Army who had an observation post on top of the town municipal building. The couple guessed that the Japanese Army would never bother them since the Japanese Army observed, with their binoculars from the top of the town municipal building, their daily activities around the house and concluded that they were civilians and the Guerrilla Soldiers never patronized their place.

Devoid of the Japanese Army harassments, the Filipino civilians devoted their daily activities to agriculture, and the rice harvests of September, 1943 was bountiful and Damaso had high expectation of more food production during the succeeding months except for apprehensions that the Japanese Army would confiscate the rice grains. The old man excavated a rectangular pit under his house and lined the earthen walls with wooden planks and bamboo tree slats and funneled the grains into the silo; replacing the ground flooring of his house, he hid the supply as safely as he thought until the October rain fell. The old man checked on his stash and found to his horror that the rice grain silo was flooded, so he scooped the palay grains with pails and baskets, from the bottom of the pit, aware that an hour of delay meant unpalatable cereal food. The grains were dried under the heat of the sun but the acrid and powdery grains lost much of their palatability. The supply lasted until the first quarter of 1944 when it was planting season time. The rice fields were readied for planting and Damaso soaked, the last two sacks of palay, which he would use as seedlings, in water as germinating-hastening process before the seeds, were broadcasted the following day. The hundred heads of fowls were likewise fenced in a poultry pen, the night before, preventing the poultry from feeding on the broadcasted seedlings the following day, and the old man retired for the night thinking of the busy day ahead.

Howling of the dogs unsettled the tranquility of the night while footsteps harbingered the approaches of the nocturnal visitors, and then loud knockings on the wooden door awakened the tired old man who reluctantly opened the door and the armed strangers barged inside the house. They searched everywhere and took everything they could lay their hands on. The hostile intruders took all the clothing, except those worn by the house occupants, the sacks of palay seeds, a barrel of sugar, rice grains, and hauled away all the fowls from the poultry pen. The intruders poked at, with pointed stake, every foot of the ground around the house and dug out the china wares that were buried in the ground; while the old man stood aside dejectedly and helpless at the arrogance and greed of his countrymen. Neighbors opined that the predators were Guerrilla Soldiers; others believed that they were town thugs who turned into looters, while others insisted they were neighbors living at a distance who turned into thieves. Whoever they were, their acts were nemesis of food production and abettors of starvation. Thieves plucked out corn ears before the silken tassels knotted down, peanuts, sweet potatoes, and cassavas were uprooted before they matured. The Filipino Civilians fed on buds of sugar cane, cores of banana stalks, and wild roots that were ridden of poison. Work animals were threatened of extinction because farmers butchered them rather than forfeit them to the commandeerers. Food production came to a halt because the farmers were threatened from the Japanese Army, the fellow Civilians and the Guerrilla Soldiers.

The Guerrilla domains were incapable of food production because the hills, the mountains and the forest yielded scanty food products or none at all for the subsistence of the highlanders. The Guerrilla Soldiers foraged food from the lowlands of Negros Islands and transported the food supply by caravan of haulers to the mountain depots; the quantities were dependent upon the availability of the crops from the plains. Thousands of the food haulers, who traveled on foot over rugged terrains of the mountains, died due to exhaustion, pneumonia, and malaria without the benefits of medicines and medications.

The river crossings at Sitio Capilian and Sitio Inambacan of my southern Defense Line linked the lowlands and highlands in the procurement of food supply. Sitio Bulad in Barrio Cansilayan was a mattress of rice land and the production of rice, a staple food, was bountiful, when combined with the production of Sitio Mining and other arable areas in Barrio Abuanan, Sitio Bulad was the rice granary nearest to my Defense Line perimeter. My Command Posts which stringed from Barrio Sumag, a Japanese Army zone, to my Rear Command Post in the mountains of the Guerrilla zone, served as observation centers in monitoring the Japanese Army movements. I encouraged the farmers in the areas, in the production of more food while I assured them of protection against the Japanese Army molestations. I instructed the farmers on feeding Guerrilla Soldiers with whatever food available on hand if the Guerrilla Soldiers passed by their way; however, impossible demands by anyone should be reported to the nearest Command Post and the complaint forwarded to my Rear Command Post with assurances of prompt action. My Headquarters at Sitio Egtalinga had an Officer on duty, twenty-four hours a day, who acted in my behalf. As precautionary measures against the Japanese Army confiscation of the harvests, the farmers transported their palay produce across Bago River where they left their products lying everywhere without fear of loss from thievery. The farmers were alerted of the Japanese Army raids into their areas and their safety from harm of the Japanese Soldiers accounted for the steady food supply to my Rear Command Post at Sitio Egtalinga, and the food shipments were eventually forwarded to the Division Headquarters up the mountain sides.

The thousands of farmers who lived in the areas of Barrio Cansilayan, Barrio Sumag, and Barrio Abuanan were my loyal Filipino Civilian supporters who made it possible for my Guerrilla Band into waging battles with the Japanese Forces. Joaquin Villarosa, a physician, contributed the produce of his farmland in Barrio Sumag to my Guerrilla Band in support of our struggle for freedom, aside from his services as Surgeon to my Guerrilla Soldiers. Hieroteo Villarosa, a lawyer, donated numerous sacks of palay for my Guerrilla movement for the cause of liberty, aside from serving as my Legal Counsel who snatched me from the abyss of my military career. Isidro Villarosa sent bulk of his hacienda production for the sustenance of my Guerrilla Soldiers, and Ana Villarosa gave liberally her farm harvests to my Guerrilla

Soldiers in furtherance of our resistance to the Japanese Army. The Araneta family who owned Hacienda Bangco and Hacienda Romualdez contributed liberally their crops in support of my Guerrilla Band in our pursuit of protection against the Japanese Forces, and Francisco Rojas tendered his crops from his hacienda for the subsistence of my Guerrilla Soldiers.

It was ironic that the Japanese Army supported the Guerrilla Soldiers in an indirect way when the Japanese Army sent Japanese spies reconnoitering Barrio Cansilayan, and the Japanese spies brought up an idea of the Japanese Army establishing a Garrison in Barrio Cansilayan. I coached the barrio populace into enumerating to the Japanese spies, the disadvantages of establishing a Japanese Army Garrison near the Guerrilla Soldiers lairs; the Japanese Army Garrison in Barrio Cansilayan would invite constant raids by the Guerrilla Soldiers from across Bago River. The ambushes and attacks by the Guerrilla Soldiers would convert Barrio Cansilayan and its environs into a no-man's land and food production would ultimately come to a stop. Without the presence of the Japanese Army in Barrio Cansilayan, food production would intensify and sufficient food would find its way to Bacolod City and would benefit the Japanese Army as well. The Japanese Army listened to the wisdom of my logic and accepted the counsel of the Japanese spies; the Japanese Army abandoned an idea of using Barrio Cansilayan Elementary School buildings as its Army Garrison.

Both the Japanese Army and the Guerrilla Soldiers coveted the palay harvests of Barrio Cansilayan and its environs; but most of all both wanted the possession of the five rice mill machines that processed palay grains. The production of rice involved planting, harvesting, and threshing. The final process was milling the palay grain, which would polish the palay grain into rice with the use of the rice-milling machine. The rice mill machines became important after the palay grains were threshed and dried under the heat of the sun for removing the husks and converting the palay grain into polished rice grains. I instructed the owners of the rice mill machines to dismantle the machines and keep the movable parts in different places and away from detection by the Japanese Soldiers and the Guerrilla Soldiers as well; the parts were assembled when milling and dismantled after each use. Major Uldarico Baclagon, another Guerrilla Officer, wanted the rice milling machines installed in his Headquarters up in the mountains; so he sent Sergeant Manuel Baylon for the confiscation of the machines, and Jose Tolimao, the owner of a mill appealed for my intercession. Farmers had their palay milled in Tolimao's rice mill by paying him a share of the product for his milling services, so the rice mill was Tolimao's source of livelihood. I instructed Jose Tolimao to tell Sergeant Baylon that should the Guerrilla Officers wanted the rice mill; Jose Tolimao would give up the machinery only after permission was obtained from Jorge G. Herrera, Jr. Jose Tolimao apprised Sergeant Baylon that the rice mill owners would rather risk the ire of the Guerilla Officers than violate the instructions of the Herrera Guerrilla Soldiers.

The controversy over the rice mill owners' refusal of surrendering the machinery without my approval was brought to the attention of Col. Ernesto Mata who was the Deputy Islands Commander of the Negros Islands Resistance Movement, who called me for explanation. I argued that the rice mills should be located at the lowlands where the produce was harvested; the farmers had their harvest milled promptly and availed of their shares of livelihood. Only polished rice stripped of the weight of the husks were transported up hills to the Divisional Headquarters. Colonel Ernesto Mata, Commander of the North Sector of the Negros Islands Resistance Movement and Alfredo Montelibano, Sr. Military Governor of Free Negros Islands, concurred with my opinion.

The disbandment of the USAFFE led to differences of opinions among Guerrilla Leaders at this stage of our resistance movement that hampered the Guerrilla Soldiers campaign against the Japanese Army. There were disagreements among the Guerrilla Leaders as to who would be the highest Guerrilla Officer to lead the Negros Islands Resistance Movement. The split between the Guerrilla Leaders from the Oriental side and those from the Occidental side of Negros Islands led to two sets of Guerrilla Leadership until some of the Guerrilla Leaders integrated under the leadership of Col. Salvador Abcede; others left Negros Islands.

Day and night during the harvest season, bancas shuttled back and forth at Sitio Capilian and Sitio Inambacan, transporting rice from the lowlands to the foothills at Sitio Bacong and the cereals were transshipped to the Guerrilla Division Headquarters up the mountains. I estimated that the families of the Villarosa alone contributed no less than 120,000 sacks of rice in a year for the support of the Guerrilla Resistance Movement. Hacienda Bang-co, Hacienda Romualdez and several individuals' contributions swelled the volume of my rice supply. I stored 110,000 sacks of the best variety of polished rice grain at my Bivouac in Sitio Egtalinga after the allotments of the Divisional Headquarters were shipped out. My Headquarters was an enviable barn with bins of cereals stockpiled in each storehouse. Grains of various kinds of the best varieties arrived on horsebacks; cow and carabao sleds, and women and children were kept busy in drying and storing the grains in the barns, and for their services the workers were paid in kind.

The Japanese Army raided Barrio Bacong and attempted in locating my storehouses, but they missed finding my Headquarters, and the Japanese Army never realized that the Filipino Civilians living around Barrio Bacong composed the membership of my 500-strong bolo battalion who would fight to death in defense of the storehouses under my command. At Sitio Inambacan, there was a 200-foot high cliff on top of which was a cave overlooking Bago River. Trusted Filipino Civilian supporters guarded the cave because I stored 6,000 sacks of rice of the best variety as a reserved food supply; the grains were hauled up sack by sack through a rope pulley from a banca on a river below to the cave up the cliff.

As complement to the grains, we had steady supply of fish from the river for Bago River teemed with edible marine life such as the king of all fresh water fish; the eel which measured to as large as four inches in diameter and four feet long with the least of bones. Scraped of glossy, slimy films, the eel's spotted skins changed into hoggish white; wedge-cut, sun dried and cooked over charcoal embers, it served as a delectable dish. My cook inserted the whole portion of the cleansed eel inside a bamboo and the tube was roasted over the fire; when the green bamboo tube dried and caught fire, the eel became a favorite menu garnished in green guava top leaves. The eel cleaned, salted and dried under the heat of the sun, were preserved for days as food supply. Next to eels as special catch of Bago River were other native fish differentiated by their appearances, sizes, and tastes such as: *tadloñgan*, which resembled grayling; *bulan-bulan*, Rudd; *akikiro*, sea water hatchet; *bagtis*, brown trout; and *ubog*, trench. *Banagan*, *locon* and *pahî* were lobsters, shrimps and prawns. The *bonogs* were fresh water anchovies while awis were fresh water edible shells.

At waist-deep portion of Bago River in Barrio Antipuluan, bamboo fish trap sifted the river for fish. Bamboo posts and beams supporting whole length of bamboo poles were matted alongside each other and spread 35 degrees tangent to the river-bed. A round log, a yard in diameter, pinned down on the river bed one ends of the poles and accentuated the abrupt fall of the water current over the log and into the bamboo flooring of the fish trap. Bamboo fences extending side ways and forward from the terminals of the log, served as funnels that guided the water current and the fish into the floors of the bamboo fish trap. On dry season, the catch was sparse, but rainy days swelled the turbulence, and the murky water blinded the aquatic creatures, the strong water current carried them along and dumped them into the flooring of the fish trap. With sacks in hand, the fish trap watchers had a heyday collecting the flailing fish into the bags. The fish trap Owner who was a Guerrilla Movement supporter and his Overseer who was my undercover agent placed the fish catches at my disposal.

The steady supply of rice and fish provided my Guerrilla Soldiers ample supply of food, and my Scouts who doubled as food procurers carried sufficient amount of cash in payment for food we procured from other sources or to those who served food to us while we were out of the Command Posts on combat missions. The supporters and sympathizers of the Guerrilla movement, in many instances refused our proffer of cash compensation for their food and catering services on their logic that "if we feed soldiers who 'eat and run' then there was no reason why we should never feed these group of soldiers who 'hit and run' if we were to treat fairly these group of soldiers." The truth of the matter was that we also ran, after the battle engagements for purposes of conservation of our limited supply of arms and ammunitions, but we dealt the Japanese Army lethal blows before we disengaged from battle encounters. The Japanese Army never overlooked the counter harassments we waged against them; the Japanese Army set up entrapments for my capture, dead or alive.

CHAPTER 8

❋

Japanese Army Spies

The Japanese Imperial Forces launched a policy of attraction and billed their propaganda as "East Asian Co-prosperity Sphere" program. Filipinos were mustered into associations for purposes of fostering close cooperation between the Filipino Civilians and the Japanese Soldiers. "KALIBAPI" identification cards were issued to the members, and the tags vested on the Wearers status symbol of close affinity with the Japanese Soldiers and loyalty to the Japanese Army; the Passports exempted the beneficiaries from arrests, searches and seizures.

Felix Benitez who was an acquaintance but who elected collaboration with the Japanese Army, solicitously procured for me the KALIBAPI, making me a Guerrilla Leader with a Japanese Army visa, and suggested to me that I surrender to the Japanese Army Headquarters in Bacolod City by using the KALIBAPI as my safe conduct pass and he assured me of an unconditional pardon from the Japanese Imperial Army. I learned that no Filipino had ever reined in the Japanese Army, so I took Felix Benitez' solicitude with a grain of salt and tacked the KALIBAPI passport to the walls of my secret *nipa* hut.

In Murcia, a Japanese Army spy sent hundreds of innocent Filipino heads rolling down into excavations, for "Ogis" secured employment from Captain Sato, a Japanese Army commander of the Garrison, and spied for the Japanese Army among the

Filipino Civilians in the town. Ogis betted heavily and lost on gambling, and avenging for his losses, pointed at the winners, to the Japanese Soldiers, as members of the Guerrilla organization. The Japanese Army swallowed Ogis' lies, hook, line and sinker, and arrested the victims who repaid Ogis with their lives when the Japanese Army executed them to death. Rosendo Hermosura earned thousands if not millions of Japanese money for his espionage services. The phrase "tanglâ sa laṅgit[25]" became a notoriously dreadful phrase during the height of World War II in the town of Murcia because the term referred to the Japanese Army mode of executing their culprits to death. The Japanese Soldiers marched their captives across the Laṅgub Creek to the avocado orchard at the northern side of the town in Hacienda Binitin where the victims were forced at digging their own graves among the avocado trees. The Japanese Executioners, using the sharpened samurai sword, chopped the heads off the captives while they were kneeling and pleading for mercy; the severed heads just tumbled down and fell into the pit, facing skyward; and many others with their hands tied behind their backs, were buried alive up to their necks that were left sticking out of their own excavations. They died facing skyward while pleading for mercy from heaven. The executions reached their peaks when the beheadings went on day and night for months without let up until death tolls reached over hundreds of dead human beings.

In Barrio Sumag, the market stallholders were surprised at the sudden fortune of Trinidad who was merely a vendor of tobacco in the market place; but who suddenly became a tobacco leaf dealer, which required a larger amount of financing, and the sources of her capital fund became the subject of speculations among the merchants in the market place. There was a suspicion that Trinidad was in the payroll of the Japanese Army, and the roster of the Japanese Army spies that reached my Command Post contained her name, so I dispatched Elpidio Macasa, one of my Soldiers, for the arrest of the suspect who was brought to Sitio

---

25. Negros Islands phrase which literally meant, "face skyward".

Kipot, a subcommand post for questioning. Trinidad was subjected to a thorough investigation, which yielded a negative result; on other hand, the investigation disclosed that her competitors who wanted her out of business framed up Trinidad. Trinidad transferred her business elsewhere.

In Sitio Maasin, the hacienda Overseer enticed me with a palay donation, so the Overseer and I set up an appointment and a date for the hauling of the donation to my Guerrilla hideout. The Japanese Army and the Overseer, on the other hand, contrived an elaborate plan of springing a trap of my Soldiers, so at the appointed time, the Japanese Army surrounded the warehouse with well-entrenched soldiers who waited for our entrance into their trap; however, I accepted the donation and hauled them three days ahead of the appointed date to the disappointment of the Japanese Army. The land owner, himself, sided with the Japanese Army and he dressed in the Japanese Army tattered uniforms underneath a ramie sack that hid his entire body except for his eyes, ears, nose and mouth that were provided with portholes, and his arms that protruded out of the holes of a sack. The masquerade altered his identity while he moved in Barrio Sumag and the surrounding areas in his spying activities with the Japanese Army. Many Filipino Civilians lost their lives as a result of his connivance with the Japanese Army and the Guerrilla Soldiers seemed helpless at taking him out of his spying business because he was well-entrenched and well-protected by the Japanese Soldiers.

From the south, Manuel Bamba who resided from the town of La Carlota posed a grave danger to the Guerrilla Resistance Movement when he set a goal for himself, the liquidation of key Guerrilla Leaders on behalf of the Japanese Army, and my name headed his list. Roaming around in the country sides and leaving deaths in his wakes to the delight of the Japanese Army, Manuel Bamba proved to be a challenge to the Resistance Movement. I studied his movements and I analyzed carefully his *modus operandi,* which consisted of the use of horses for speedy transportation and communication with the Japanese Army. I was tipped off of his coming to Barrio Abuanan, so I lined up incognito my Soldiers along his path, and sure enough, the galloping black stallion, loaned to him by millionaire Don Jose Soriano of La Castellana, augured his approach while I rode on a staid horse on our "chance" encounter. From a shouting distance, Manuel Bamba boasted of his luck in meeting me by chance.

"I had been looking for you all over the places, Jorge, am I now glad that you are in my hands?" Manuel Bamba chuckled with a glee of success.

The physically, powerfully-built Manuel Bamba was so confident of himself that he felt he could break my skinny neck with his bare hands, and he drew his revolver with the aim of killing me in an instant; however, he proved too slow and I unleashed the firepower of my .45 Cal. Handgun before Manuel Bamba could ever touch his gun's trigger. I hit Manuel Bamba on his forehead, and he flew off his horse and he slumped limply to the ground where I rushed to his side, but the fatal shots cut short our conversation; Manuel Bamba died on the spot, giving up his life for a wrong cause.

The Japanese Army farmed out spies into all directions towards my position in the hills across Bago River and the Japanese Army undercover agents posed as farm laborers, farmers, traders, evacuees and returning residents; residents of the Barrios who opted residing in Bacolod City and who pretended coming back to their Barrio homes. They took run-about routes from Barrio Sumag and the town of Murcia with Barrio Cansilayan as their main destination. The intrepid ones took a more direct route starting from Barrio Mansiliñgan, skirted Sitio Maasin and Sitio Jovellanos, and ended at Sitio Bulad. From Sitio Bulad in Barrio Cansilayan, only Bago River separated them from my Rear Command Post.

The pattern of the Japanese Army espionage operations surfaced; the spies got lost in the mix of the mainstream of the Filipino Civilians with a major objective. They identified as many Guerrilla Soldiers in the area as they could uncover, and in an opportune time, called in the Japanese Soldiers who moved in fast for the capture of the Guerrilla Soldiers. The raids might be conducted in broad daylight or at nighttime when their quarries got so complacent that they were caught unprepared for escape; the Japanese Soldiers closed in stealthily and swiftly with successes. The Japanese Army raids were always preceded by the penetration and the encasement of the targeted areas by the Japanese Army spies, and in a delicate espionage missions, the Japanese Army had its spies devised elaborate schemes at bagging prized Guerrilla Leaders.

Jose Tesoro was one of the Japanese Army spies who undertook special espionage missions for the Japanese Army. A native of Barrio Cansilayan, Jose Tesoro moved to Bacolod City when Roque Tesoro, his father, became the Chief of Police of Bacolod City under the Japanese Army Puppet Government, and on several occasions, Jose Tesoro sojourned back to Barrio Cansilayan; his frequent visits to the Barrio raised eyebrows of suspicions. It did take a long time before I came into grip with him, and the morning I learned that he was in his relative's house, I sent Jose Lo and Jose Diaz, my Soldiers, for his apprehension. Jose Tesoro denied vigorously his relationship with the Japanese Army and protested vehemently his arrest, but the two Guerrilla Soldiers stood pat on my instructions.

"We regret very much," the Guerrilla Soldiers explained, "but we have orders of taking you along with us, whether you are dead or alive."

Standing before the nozzles of gun barrels, Jose Tesoro had no choice other than submission. I had him brought to my Command Post at Sitio Bulad. The following day of his capture, being a market day in Barrio Bacong, the sight of Jose Tesoro in our possession, might be known to the market goers who might, in turn, alert the Japanese Army, so I ushered Jose Tesoro into a nipa hut in Sitio Bulad where I conducted an investigation.

"Why do you keep coming back to Barrio Cansilayan when your family stays in Bacolod City?" I started the inquiry.

Jose Tesoro reasoned out that during harvest season, he wanted more stocks of grains.

"Is it not a fact that there is abundant supply of rice grains in Bacolod City? Why bother yourself with the harvests from Barrio Cansilayan?"

Jose Tesoro offered lame excuses and I wanted them belied. I wanted to puncture his walls of alibi and prove him a liar while I pricked on his conscience into exacting an admission of guilt. I wanted a change in his conviction and his probable conversion as an asset of the Guerrilla Resistance Movement; I wanted his intimate relationship with the Japanese Army utilized into providing me an invaluable ally inside the Japanese Army organization, who could supply me with vital war information.

"Did not the Japanese Army coach you on the answers you must provide if questioned by the Guerrilla Soldiers?"

He ignored my insinuations.

"Was not your father summoned to the Japanese Army Headquarters for a conference and report every time you arrived from your spying missions from Barrio Cansilayan?"

The suspect remained silent.

"Did not your father and the Japanese Army plot your entry into Barrio Cansilayan and my eventual capture?"

Jose Tesoro shook his head.

"Don't you know that every word that was exchanged between your father and the Japanese Soldiers regarding your spying missions in Barrio Cansilayan had been closely monitored by us?"

I expected that Jose Tesoro would confess everything he was and knew; instead he denied all my allegations; so I pulled out the last trump of cards against him.

"To illustrate to you my easy access to Bacolod City, how would you like reuniting with your wife at noontime?" I queried him, half expecting an answer.

Shortly before noon, my Soldiers arrived in Sitio Bulad with Jose Tesoro's wife in tow. I billeted them in a hut near my Command Post and I placed them under close guard. Jose Tesoro proved to have been made of sterner stuff than I expected of a man under the same circumstances with the presence of his wife in a dangerous situation, instead of concern, he hinted of an eventual deliverance by the Japanese Army.

The disappearance of Jose Tesoro, a Japanese Army star spy, and the concern of Roque Tesoro over the safety of his son, as well as the Japanese Army anxiety over the outcome of a well-laid out plan for my capture, raised considerable alarm. I brought along with me Jose Tesoro to my Command Post at Sitio Kipot in an effort of dramatizing before Jose Tesoro his helplessness in the hands of the Guerrilla Soldiers. The Japanese Army mounted a rescue operation, and late at dusk, two truckloads of Japanese Soldiers arrived at Barrio Sumag bound for Barrio Cansilayan. A Japanese Army armored car led the convoy that paraded 20 meters in front of my Soldiers who were well-concealed and in a position for possible battle encounter. I dared Jose Tesoro yell for succor from his father who was riding on the Japanese Army lead car and whose voice was heard rising over the din of flurries of the Japanese Army Patrol. Jose Tesoro froze in terror at the sight of guns aimed at his temples until the Japanese Army Patrol passed by our position. The presence of the Filipino Civilians in the area prevented us from the ambush of the Japanese Army Soldiers.

I placed Jose Tesoro under close guard at Sitio Bulad, hoping for a complete change of his attitude and Jose Tesoro went along with my ideas; he volunteered for household errands, an encouraging outward manifestation of his transformation. One of his tasks was fetching potable water from a well that had been dug out of the Sumag River bank, and Abner Dequiña escorted him on his daily rounds of errand between the hut and the river. While he balanced the bamboo poles with two empty kerosene cans dangling wildly from both ends of the pole, a sinister plan of escape from his captors hatched in Jose Tesoro's intractable mind, and walking down the steep and winding his way on a narrow path between the slopes of the riverbank, Jose Tesoro threw back his loads so suddenly that the pole and the cans crashed into the faces of his escort. He lunged for the gun and wrestled with Abner Dequiña for the possession of the weapon, but he overlooked a cardinal principle in the handling of a rifle; the difficulty of disarming a guard whose rifle sling was wrapped around the guard's forearm. Abner Dequiña pulled the trigger and the bullet found its mark in Jose Tesoro's chest. I was summoned to the hut where I found Jose Tesoro lying in a pool of his blood; his wounds were bleeding profusely. I reiterated to Jose Tesoro the good intention I stored for him if only he would amend his spying ways and collaborate with the Guerrilla Soldiers, but Jose Tesoro stuck to the righteousness of his conviction up to the last gasp of his breath; and I lost a distant relative to the cause of the Japanese Army.

The Japanese Army recalled its top undercover agent from the north, and sent her into tracking me down. The female Japanese Army undercover agent went to work immediately at a brisk pace. She lodged with the Tughap family, the evacuees who lived along the Sumag River bank at Sitio Bulad; a hundred meters away, integrated herself among the residents of Barrio Cansilayan, and groped her way across Bago River to Barrio Bacong posing as one of the traders from Bacolod City. Her main objective as she intimated to the curious bystanders whom she approached for assistance for directions, was a meeting with Jorge G. Herrera, Jr. The barrio residents, whom Gloria Alvaran questioned, explained to her that Herrera hid in the mountain fastnesses but came oftentimes down to Barrio Bacong; and the residents advised Gloria Alvaran into sticking out around the Barrio for a chance meeting. Gloria honed on her homework well, and she spent time roving around Barrio Bacong and gathering as much information as she could about my movements. After a week of her presence in Barrio Bacong, I decided on administering an initial probing of her purposes, so I posed as one of the evacuees in the Barrio approached her and I asked Gloria if she knew Jorge G. Herrera, Jr. in person.

"Can you recognize Jorge G. Herrera, Jr. if you see him?" I inquired impersonally.

"Yes, I know him intimately." Gloria Alvaran ended the interview.

Weeks later, I granted Gloria Alvaran an audience in my Rear Command Post when my Soldier ushered her into my Headquarters in Sitio Egtalinga.

"He is the Jorge G. Herrera, Jr. that you were looking for. Have you seen him before?" My Soldiers pointed her way towards my direction and left without waiting for her reply.

Whatever emotion seized Gloria Alvaran in my presence, she never betrayed outwardly. Gloria failed the initial test, but she made up for her failure with a guile of a woman. In her mid-twentieth, Gloria Alvaran was as beautiful as any typical Filipino and her womanliness belied an evil heart inside her well-proportioned feminine figure. Her scheming mind was equal to the task of espionage assigned to her by the Japanese Army and her cunning head was a hard nut to crack. She vehemently denied her bond with the Japanese Army and she rationalized her presence in Barrio Bacong as purely for commerce and amity.

"Do you realize the consequences of offering your services to the Japanese Army?" I attempted at tripping her off balance into admission.

"You will be killing thousands of Guerrilla Soldiers and Filipino Civilians," I paused for effect, but Gloria Alvaran kept silent.

"Why do you take sides with the Japanese Army? You must remember that the Japanese Army will never countenance treachery; if you betray your countrymen, the Japanese Army will suspect that you will be apt to betraying its confidence, and the Japanese Army may execute you to death in the final analysis." I reminded Gloria.

"What will you obtain from the Japanese Army that the Guerrilla Soldiers will never grant you? We have ample supply of food, we lay our hands on anything we wanted from Bacolod City, and we have lots of fun in the mountainsides as we hold dances at anytime we wanted to. All I ask of you is the severance of your ties from the Japanese Army and your full cooperation with the Guerrilla Soldiers."

Gloria Alvaran turned deaf ears to my harangues.

"You may attempt an escape from this territory, but I must dissuade you against such an idea for your every movement is under surveillance and your every step is being watched. You will never reach the sanctuary of the Japanese Army because; death will stalk every inch of your journey back to treachery." I warned Gloria Alvaran.

Days of probation and proffer of inducements for Gloria Alvaran's change of heart passed and I almost gave up hope of ever converting her into an ally. I was to prove to her that she was a Japanese Army spy before I could convince her into joining our side, so I administered the final examination. I convened all competent females to my Headquarters and briefed them thoroughly on the objectives of the scrutiny. They were to undress, in private, Gloria Alvaran and search for the Japanese character, which was supposedly the identifying mark of the Japanese Army spies. The women were to localize the search of the mark on Gloria Alvaran's body including the inner recesses of her private vital parts.

The explorations exposed a brand etched on her skin on top of the pelvic bone; but when confronted of the findings, Gloria Alvaran insisted that the figure was a birthmark. The symbol approximated a flattened grape; the top of the fruit resembled the shoulders of a human being with two lines dangling as limbs. Below the oval-shaped symbol were other lines that branched in representation of human feet. The figure was a Japanese character and I pressed Gloria Alvaran for a satisfactory explanation of the odd figure; and then Gloria Alvaran broke down and she confessed. She was hired by the Japanese Army as a spy, she was sent to my hideouts for the identification, the monitor of my movements, and would engineer my capture by the Japanese Army. As remuneration for the success of my entrapment and capture, the Japanese Army promised Gloria Alvaran a handsome cash reward of TWO MILLIONS Japanese money. At last, Gloria Alvaran saw her way through clearly; she turned into a new leaf, embraced the tenets of the Resistance Movement and she survived the War.

Unknown to Gloria Alvaran, her intrusion into the Guerrilla territory was a set-up and a well-conceived plan plotted by my Japanese Army Counter Spy whom I planted inside the Japanese Army Headquarters in Bacolod City. It was the suggestion of my undercover Agent to the Japanese Army that led to the recall of Gloria Alvaran and for her reassignment to my capture; our purpose was the elimination of a very effective Japanese Army Spy. They were the Guerrilla Soldiers who formed the relay from Bacolod City to Sitio Bulad and they were the Guerrilla Soldiers who conducted Gloria Alvaran to another secret Agent, the Tughap family, who provided her shelter. The strangers from whom Gloria Alvaran made inquiries relayed the details of Gloria Alvaran's activities to my Headquarters; her passage was a one-way trip into the hands of the Guerrilla Soldiers.

The secret of my successes against the Japanese Army spies lay in the hands of the Filipino Civilians who lived in my Guerilla territory for each person functioned as an undercover agent who was supportive of my fighting band. The Filipino Civilians identified every stranger and extracted details of the strangers' activities for transmission to my Command Post. Even the invalids and the aged people who preferred meeting, head-on, the Japanese Army rather than evasion, played a welcoming party role to the delight of the Japanese Soldiers; but they misled the Japanese Soldiers and they extracted vital information relevant to the movement of the Japanese Army Patrol and the safety of the population. I executed to death no less than 50 Japanese Army spies with the aid of my loyal supporters; but the starring role in the espionage drama with the Japanese Army, was reserved to BLACKHAWK.

CHAPTER 9

Lost Horizon

Next of importance to the human resources in our resistance against the Japanese Army, were the natural barriers of Negros Islands, which proved to be the nemesis of the Japanese Imperial Forces. The Philippines, an archipelago of more than 7,100 islands and islets, lying 805 kilometers in the northeastern coast of Asia, had a land area of 186,405 square kilometers; bounded on the east by the Philippine Sea; on the south by the Celebes Sea; and on the north and west by the China Sea. It stretched 1,700 kilometers from Batan Island in the north to Sulu Island in the south; and 900 kilometers east to west at its widest width, but only 137 islands had an area of more than a square kilometer. This island nation grouped into Luzon Island with an area of 65,048 square kilometers; Mindoro, 5,692; and Palawan, 1,713, comprising the island group in its northern and western flanks; Mindanao Island, 58,799 square kilometers to its southern extremity; and the Visayan Islands, in its central and eastern sides, which consisted of Bohol, 2,369 square kilometers; Cebu, 1,740; Leyte, 4,484; Masbate, 2,032; Samar, 8,138; Panay, 7,155; and Negros Islands with a land area of 7,322 square kilometers.

Negros Islands[26] which shaped like a discarded jungle boot lay

---

26 Negros Islands was a political merger and designation of Negros Island and the neighboring Siquijor Island.

washed in the Visayan Sea southeast of Manila, the capital city of the nation, in Luzon Island. From the small town of Cadiz and halfway the width of the Island's northern extremity, an imaginary straight line stretched 200 kilometers off center towards the cuboids of the boot at the town of Basay at its southern extremity. The width of the Imaginary Line was approximately eight kilometers of juggernauts of mountain ranges, hills, rivers, streams, creeks, canyons, gorges, mounds, and ravines which posed formidable obstacles to anyone's trek from the northern to the southern ramparts of Negros Islands. Traveling from one mountain to another was no mean feat but an arduous task for there was no way of forging a straight line but routes of rounding the peaks, descending, ascending, and retracing one's way back and forth in a seemingly short distance between two points. A local phrase "Do Ol Ra" became a familiar joke among us, for Negros Islands was geographically divided into two provinces: Negros Occidental on the west with its Ilonggo dialect-speaking population and Negros Oriental on the east with its Cebuano dialect-speaking populace. The phrase "Do Ol Ra" was a Cebuano dialect phrase, which signified a degree of nearness, the way an Englishman would indicate a proximate location with "It's around the bend" expression. A mountaineer from the eastern Negros Islands, when queried on how far the next mountain was, would invariably turn his back towards the traveler's direction and in deadpan seriousness would point ahead and would reply "Do Ol Ra". A traveler could only curse his breath or laugh out his frustrations at the realization of an endless walk without ever reaching the next hill; yet when he met another stranger on the way, he could never resist the temptation of asking the same question knowing in advance that he would obtain the same reply. The phrase spoken by a stranger to harried traveler wrought magic somehow, for it assuaged taut nerves and rubbed out weary sinews.

An initial challenge to a traveler's journey from the north came from a mountain 3,140 feet above sea level at the outskirt of Cadiz, and if the traveler continued his southern sojourn, he

would reach another summit standing 4,137 feet between Sitio
Isidro and the town of Escalante east of the boundary. The rugged terrain progressed to an ascent 4,602 feet at Sitio Hiyang-hi-
yang which the lowlanders referred to as a point nearer to heav-
en than anywhere else and where the lowlanders jokingly would
prefer a local call rather than avail of an expensive long-distance
telephone call to heaven. It was of course, a *raison d'etre*, a con-
soling thought for a hardy traveler who arduously clung to rocks
and tree roots on the way up the mountains and slid down, literally, on the seat of his pants. The ranges broadened into a series of mounts as if offering respite to a resolute rover only to
encounter a challenge of a 464-foot hill, the highest in the prai-
ries that parted Sitio Dos Hermanos (west) from Sitio Malabago
(east) of the political boundary; and then, the summit catapult-
ed to 4,820 feet, the crest that overlooked Barrio Granada in
Bacolod City, the capital of Negros Occidental; and collectively
the mountain ranges from the town of Cadiz to Barrio Granada
became known as the Marapara Mountains. The rugged slopes
broadened into plateaus of Barrio Buenavista, Barrio Sta. Rosa,
Barrio Pandanon, and Barrio San Miguel that served as mountain pass linking Bacolod City to the west from the town of San
Carlos in the east. The outskirt of San Carlos itself squatted on
an elevation of 492 feet above sea level until it joined the lineal
boundary to the south.

The foot of the Negros Islands boot was pock marked with
mountain ranges as the distance closed in from south to north.
Cloistered west of the boundary, the town of Nonas had 1,200
feet elevation, Caliling's forested height was 1,350 feet, and the
town of Cartagena had an elevation of 1,390 feet above sea level.
Between the towns of Sipalay and Hinobaan, the areas peaked
at 1,113 feet and 1,439 feet. On the eastern side of Negros Islands, a triangle described by the towns of Catalina, Lake Balin-
sayao and Siaton was the site of mountains of 1,683, 2,574, and
696-foot high elevation, respectively, while the tallest elevation
between Sitio Baloc-baloc and Sitio San Antonio was 5,700 feet.
Among the coastal towns that acted as buffers between the sea

and the prominent peaks in the eastern section of Negros Islands were: Manjuyud, 2,652 feet; Ayuñgon, 1,782 feet; while
Tambo area had 1,536 feet; Bandoy, 2,383 and another 2,674 feet
high elevation extended towards Tambo area and abutted the
north-south boundary. Libertad had 2,253 feet high elevation;
Gihulñgan, 2,973; and Basak 2,049 feet tall. Sojourners claimed
that traveling from Basay, the southern fringes of Negros Islands
through the boundary ranges from south to north, and between
Candoni, the western, and Mabinay the eastern edges of Negros
Islands; the longitudinal sojourn of Negros Islands enveloped by
thick rain forests, deprived the travelers of even a glitter of sun
rays for weeks even during the sunniest days of the year. Of the
tallest mountain peaks were: Tabo, a matter of 349 feet; but the
succeeding mounts between Suay and Libertad rose to 3,729 feet
above sea level. The mountain barrier between Isabela-Libas and
Basak culminated to a peak of 2,434 feet high with the tallest
of all the Negros Islands mountains, the Mount Canlaon that
poked proudly at 8,080 feet above sea level and a volcano crater
on its top; and while, the Marapara Mountains composed the
northern mountain ranges, Canlaon Mountains encompassed
all the summits towards the south.

Wild denizens roamed the breath and width of the wilderness of Negros Islands; the rustling of leaves, the shaking of tree
branches and the swaying of rattan vines presaged the shadowy
approaches of the simians. The monkeys assaulted, battered, and
carried off to death human intruders, while hordes of stamped-
ing wild boars dug up corpses and scattered the scrapped skulls
in their wakes; the wild swine scented the presence of human beings kilometers away, and they enveloped their quarry into submission and death and they feasted on the corpses. Pythons laid
in wait, like fallen logs, for their unsuspecting preys. I walked,
once on foot, on a span across a creek and when I came back, I
noticed that I was standing on the most crooked branch of a tree
I had ever seen in my life; and just then the span moved and I
realized that I was standing on a python that forded the creek, so
I ran to safety. The snakes were deadly adversaries, although the

Philippine cobras were no more than a couple of feet long, yet they reared their ugly heads, and their lethal pangs, with deadly venoms, dug into human flesh when trodden on, and the victims died in less than a day's time if left unattended to by physicians. Leeches flung like hail of tiny darts into human skin, sucking human being of his blood, but I discovered an effective way of evading them; passing among them at the wee hours of the morning when they were still inactive. Even vegetation conspired in the slaying of human intruders into the jungle, for unknown to many trespassers, there were specie of tall trees that released matured and dried fruits; the pods of the fruits dropped like pebble bombs and the flailing caudal appendages of the pods kept the missiles on target into human skulls that strayed underneath the jungle trees. It was an open secret that thousands of the Filipino Civilians who were recruited as food and arms haulers, and who were unfamiliar of the dangers of the forest died on the way over the mountain ranges. Many of the Filipino haulers hardly made a one-way trip when they perished as a result of wild animal assaults, jungle fever, pneumonia, malaria, fatigue, starvation, and of hidden potent jungle killers. Scores were buried in the waysides; and hundreds more were dumped over the cliff into the earth's bosoms. The mountain ranges of Negros Islands were repulsively hostile; which was one of the reasons why the Japanese Imperial Forces failed utterly in its subjugation of the Guerrilla Resistance Movement of Negros Islands.

Several months earlier, Honorable Alfredo Montelibano, Sr. who was the Mayor of Bacolod City when the Japanese Forces landed, left Bacolod City, as a consequence of a slapping incident over the refusal of Alfredo Montelibano full cooperation with the Japanese Army and the Japanese Army's displeasure. I received orders from the Guerrilla Resistance Movement Military Higher Command that I secure the escape route of Honorable Montelibano, so I gathered my Soldiers and proceeded to the outskirt of Bacolod City. The Japanese Forces had the monopoly of the highways and the national highway between Bacolod City and the town of Murcia was not an exception. I deployed strategically my fully armed Soldiers along the 17-kilometer stretch of the road with the purpose of delaying any Japanese Army pursuit or annihilating any pursuing Japanese Soldiers if the situation demanded. I posted covertly the rest of my Soldiers on both flanks of Mr. Montelibano's party during their exodus from Bacolod City to Hacienda Binitin, his farmland in Murcia, which served as an intermediary during his escape to the mountains of Negros Islands. A truckload of Japanese Soldiers emerged and headed towards our direction and my Soldiers stirred into attacking position, but we let the Japanese Patrol passed by when I sensed that the Japanese Soldiers were unaware of the ongoing escape of Honorable Montelibano.

Several months after Mr. Montelibano escape from Bacolod City, he dissuaded Major Ernesto Mata from leaving Negros Islands for Luzon Island, and convinced the Major into organizing the Negros Islands Resistance Movement while Honorable Alfredo Montelibano, Sr. headed the Free Negros Islands Government as its Military Governor. The reorganization of the Negros Islands Resistance Movement would follow later when Colonel Salvador Abcede headed the Negros Islands Resistance Movement as the Negros Islands Commander and at the same time Division Commander of the Southern Negros Sector, while Major Ernesto Mata was selected as his Deputy and at the same time Division Commander of North Negros Sector.

I was summoned to the office of Honorable Alfredo Montelibano, Sr., the Military Governor of Free Negros Islands, instructing me into proceeding to Free Bago, an entry point to the seat of the Government of Free Negros Islands which was located in an undisclosed location in the mountains, which was designated merely as the "LOST HORIZON" or the "AERIE'S NEST" so-called perhaps, in a painstaking effort of pinpointing the specific area among the fastnesses of the vast mountain ranges of Negros Islands. I took along with me Cesar Sarito, my trusted Soldier, and together we threaded our way to Sitio Duguan, southwest of my Rear Command Post and dragged ourselves along the elevation towards Sitio Ulimbo, the threshold to the secret trail that led to the LOST HORIZON, where our entry was assiduously challenged, and the Guards interrogated me intensively on the purpose of my entry. When I explained that the Military Governor summoned me, the Sentries demanded pieces of evidence of the summons, which I did not possess. I presented myself for entry to the innermost sanctum of the Guerrilla Government but I could not produce an iota of documentation nor would I spell out my name as added identification. Demetrio Gallo, the Chief of Police of Free Bago and on whose shoulders fell the task of guarding the secret entry point to the path that ended into the seat of the Free Negros Islands Government was adamant in his refusal, just as I was insistent in gaining entrance. We reasoned out with each other, and if there was such thing as word war between two persons, we had it and the intensity of our arguments escalated and our debates dragged on for hours until, at last, I felt that the issues between us would be better settled at the barrels of our guns. I stressed my point in not bringing along with me any piece of document for such scrap of paper would be self-incriminating once I got captured by the Japanese Army. I prohibited anyone including my Soldiers from mentioning my name before any stranger for the purpose of concealing my identity and boosting my chances of escape if I were captured incognito by the Japanese Soldiers. I hid my identity from Guerrilla Soldiers as precaution from Guerrilla Soldiers squealing on me or leading the Japanese Soldiers to my hiding places if the Japanese Army captured them. I proposed to Demetrio Gallo, to break an impasse, that I leave Cesar Sarito, my trusted companion with Demetrio Gallo's Soldiers as my guarantee of good faith with the request that Cesar Sarito be taken good care with food; while Demetrio Gallo and I traveled together and I assumed full responsibility of explaining my presence before Honorable Alfredo Montelibano, Sr., the Military Governor. Demetrio Gallo accepted, grudgingly, my proposals, and we broke the deadlock.

Demetrio Gallo guided me into maze of tangled trails under the canopy of tangled rain forests where I felt that every descent ushered me deeper down the canyons and rivers, and every ascent propelled me into loftier heights and the craggy hills abetted my travails of groping my way along circuitous pathways under the cover of darkness of the shadows in the forests. We walked on rugged terrains; and as we scaled the mountain walls, we anchored our toes on slippery rocks and we held on to tree roots with vise-grip fingers. The jungle denizens must have been stumped at our stubbornness and they might have been sympathetic to our plights because they let us pass without a challenge during our nocturnal assaults against the labyrinth of the jungle.

Honorable Alfredo Montelibano, Sr., the Military Governor of Free Negros Islands Government, had his cabin nestled in the mountain wilderness, but his dwelling was equipped with urban facilities in an urban atmospheres which were made possible through the labor, love and loyalty of the Filipino people who opted for resistance against the Japanese Forces, rather than surrender to the Japanese Army. President Manuel L. Quezon, the first President of the Commonwealth of the Philippines under the United States Government, appointed him in 1941, the first Mayor of Bacolod City until World War II broke out.

Honorable Alfredo Montelibano, Sr. assumed the Military Governorship of Negros Islands when he risked his life in resistance to the Japanese Army, suffered hardships in the mountains rather than live a life of comfort under the Japanese Army. Honorable Alfredo Montelibano, Sr. served the Filipino nation further when President Manuel L. Quezon died while on exile in the United States and Vice President Sergio Osmeña, Sr. who succeeded President Quezon, appointed him Secretary of National Defense and Interior after the end of World War II. The first presidential election was held after the Philippines gained independence from the United States of America. It was Secretary of National Defense and Interior Alfredo Montelibano who asked President Osmeña whether he wanted victory in the election, for Secretary of the National Defense Alfredo Montelibano had the popular support of the Armed Forces of the Philippines, but President Osmeña declined the use of the military for political purposes and consequently he lost the election to President Manuel A. Roxas.

I was the Guest of the Military Governor in his mountain hideout and I was billeted in a room next to his, because it was a characteristic of him of discussing any subject at anytime, and he wanted as much information about war developments as I could apprise him of the war progress in my front. It was a great honor for me to be the Guest of Alfredo Montelibano, Sr., a great national leader, a nationalist, a patriot, and a philanthropist. He handed me a fat envelope of money as his gesture of appreciation and support to my ragtag Guerrilla Soldiers. It was, however, a very touching scene seeing Demetrio Gallo wept openly when Governor Montelibano embraced me, called me "Jorge" by my first name, and hugged me in greetings at the first time Demetrio Gallo and I meet him. Demetrio Gallo confessed to me that it was the first time in his life that he ever saw Jorge G. Herrera, Jr. in flesh after hearing so much of my name from the lips of many other Guerrilla Soldiers.

Demetrio Gallo and I retraced our footsteps back the jungle trails in the first and the last time that I ever went up the LOST HORIZON.

CHAPTER 10

Blackhawk

Policito Salazar became a relative when he married Adelfa Sarito, my relative and a sister of Cesar Sarito who was my most trusted and loyal Soldier until the end of World War II. The marriage took place shortly before World War II erupted. It was a blissful union between a young woman from the rustic town of Murcia and young man from the urban Bacolod City. They spent happy moments in Bago River where the fish trap fascinated them with bountiful catches, unmindful of the perils that lurked in the murky river. The turbulence that dazed the fish into captivity swelled in an unimaginable proportion until the swirling flood grabbed away the fish trap from its bamboo moorings and swallowed them into its depth. Policito Salazar survived the inundation, but Adelfa, his wife perished with the deluge.

Shortly after Policito Salazar's wife died, World War II broke out, and the Japanese Army landed in Bacolod City. He then sensed the dangers of a continuous residence in the City as the Japanese Army tightened its grip over the metropolis, and the Japanese Soldiers threatened the lives of the City dwellers. Policito Salazar approached me, after hearing of my nefarious activities and he narrated to me his predicaments; he wanted an affiliation with my Guerrilla Band as a combatant but he had still the responsibility of caring for his aged and ailing mother who might never survive the rigors of a fugitive's life in the jungle. He thought he would stay inside the Japanese Army territory in Bacolod City, in deference to the welfare of his parent, and weathers the war. Policito Salazar was at the crossroad of serving his personal interest and serving his Country; and I could only empathize with him as he narrated his predicaments. I shut him momentarily out of my mind as I visualized the role he could possibly play in the Resistance Movement. Policito Salazar, five-feet, five-inch tall stocky man, possessed oval faces that mellowed his sturdiness into a mien of contriteness if ever caught red-handed while committing a crime. Nature endowed him with thick set of eyelids and eyebrows, the physical features that were common to Asians, and at an age when young men sported western-style haircuts; Policito Salazar had a balding head. He slogged in his hurried gait, and to me he resembled a Japanese Soldier more than any other Filipino, so I marked him for a very special role.

The story of Blackhawk, a bird, rushed back to my memory. In the novel, the bird acquired traits that approximated the human's and Black hawk amassed with unerring accuracy, friends who proved helpful in the bird's espionage activities inside enemy territory. Blackhawk eluded enemy detection and as a courier, it delivered vital messages that wrought havoc and devastation on the enemy defenses; or was it the story of Blackhawk, an American Indian Chief who fought with his thirty or forty men and put to flight an attacking party of 300 hardy pioneers; and had completely demoralized the entire army of 2,500 militia and regulars, in defense of his territory, which inspired me into adopting a code name, "Blackhawk" as a symbol of our resistance against the Japanese Army?

I formulated a recommendation, after Policito Salazar concluded his story, and I dispatched him to Colonel Ernesto Mata who received my message. Colonel Mata questioned intensively, Policito Salazar's motivations, and convinced of his sincerity, Colonel Mata sent back his reply. It was an order addressed to all the Guerrilla Commanders of Negros Islands Resistance Movement, to turn over Policito Salazar to the Headquarters of Colonel Ernesto Mata if any Guerrilla Soldier captured Policito Salazar. Policito Salazar was granted a password for his secret affiliation with the Resistance Movement, a code – BLACKHAWK.

Blackhawk's initial assignment in Bacolod City was the procurement of medicines for the Negros Resistance Movement; he opened charge accounts with drugstores for the Free Negros Islands Government, signed the accounts on my behalf, and channeled the drugs to my Headquarters. The medicines that Blackhawk surreptitiously shipped me saved the lives of many Guerrilla Soldiers and snatched me from the jaws of death after pulmonary diseases struck me which almost drained me dry of blood.

Policito Salazar, in his high school days, proved to be a gregarious type of brat who roamed the areas of Bacolod City and in the process, acquired acquaintances and friends from all walks of life. He renewed the camaraderie of old friends, but to his dismay, he learned that many of them had cast their lots with the Japanese Army. The air of suspicion and distrust pervaded the atmospheres while each man probed the political leaning and patriotism of the other; each one mindful that exposure of one's belief might end in one's death either in the hands of the Guerrilla Soldiers or of the Japanese Soldiers. Policito Salazar discerned gradually the several individuals whom the Japanese Army employed for espionage among the Filipino Civilians in its effort at ferreting out the members of the Filipino Guerrilla Resistance Movement and their sympathizers wherever they were found or suspected of hiding. The majority of the Filipinos who lived the lives of mediocrity in the City were selfish and materialistic who offered their services as Japanese Army Spies. The Japanese Army availed of their unscrupulous services; although the Japanese Army found them unreliable; nevertheless, the discriminating Japanese Army installed them at the bottom of the espionage ladder. Many of the mercenaries ended as fodders to the cannons of the ambitious members of the Japanese Army spy ring.

Policito Salazar found his job taxing the limit of his strength and endurance as well as realized that his preoccupation was a hazardous undertaking. It was his task of informing me of the Japanese Army movements, which necessitated the delivery of messages to my Command Post at odd moments and at the quickest possible time; and in person. He discovered that the late evening time was auspicious moment of delivering messages while at the same time that he accommodated the Japanese Army demand of his presence in the City at midnight. He dashed to my Camp taking the shortest route that was available for him which meant struggling over barriers; evading ponds of water, rice fields, ditches, growth of sugar canes, tall grasses, and even the encounter with strangers whom he evaded for the purpose of secrecy of his mission while he fixed at the right direction in the delivery of his important message to me. Policito Salazar's ordeal ended when I acquired telephone set that was operated on a dry-cell battery, the communication apparatus that the sugar cane planters utilized in their contact with the sugar millers in the pre-war times. I installed the telephone system between my Subcommand Post at Sitio Sanduñgaw and my Rear Command Post at Sitio Egtalinga. The telephone lines were concealed on the tops of branches of growing wild trees along the stream from Tabucol stream to its delta in Bago River. A small hut housed the telephone set terminal and its operator at Sitio Sanduñgaw and guards who posed as wood gatherers watched over the installation. The Guards doubled also as radio operators in the receiving and transmitting of messages across Bago River to another Subcommand Post at Sitio Udag where couriers relayed messages with faster transportation, utilizing horses for the transmission of messages to the outskirt of Bacolod City. Commuters on foot, farmers, laborers and traders served as reliable media of communication while the messengers were rotated daily in avoiding familiarization of their faces; so my intelligence network grew stronger at each passing day.

Blackhawk tabulated faithfully the outcome of our battle encounters and dispatched the score to my Headquarters. Whenever there were battle skirmishes, Blackhawk made rounds of the Japanese Army hospitals and he encountered heart-rending scenes of young Japanese Soldiers weeping unashamedly while the Japanese Surgeons extracted nails, pellets, leads, and slugs from the Japanese Soldiers' bodies; the Japanese Soldiers proved to be as human as Filipino Soldiers in mortal pain.

My faith in Blackhawk's capabilities as an undercover agent strengthened although I entertained growing misgivings. He ingratiated himself to the Japanese Army in gaining favors, but paid dear lives for the rewards; he squealed on the other unworthy Japanese Army spies in a show of loyalty to the Japanese Army and a bid for the Japanese Army trusts. It was necessary offering the lives of the unscrupulous mercenaries for the cause of victory, while the Japanese Soldiers willingly executed to death those whom they found unreliable; and the exposure of the unfit earned for Blackhawk a place and a higher stature among the elites of spies from whom even ordinary Japanese Soldiers took orders. Black hawk unraveled gradually the Japanese Army strategy. The Japanese Army spies reconnoitered, a day before each Japanese Army scheduled raid, the Guerrilla domain and ascertained the presence of the Guerrilla Soldiers. The Japanese Army spies then led the Japanese Soldiers assaults on the suspected locations. Blackhawk never failed in alerting me of the impending Japanese Army raids, and he suggested that I leave behind at every flight, food supplies, after I retreated, which the Japanese Soldiers relished in setting to flames in their objective of depriving the Guerrilla Soldiers of logistics and in their frustrations upon their failure at capturing the Guerrilla Soldiers. Blackhawk urged me into putting up a token semblance of resistance and dispelling suspicion of leaks in the Japanese Army war plans. Blackhawk's espionage role expanded until he became privy to the discussions inside the Japanese Army Intelligence Bureau on matters pertaining to the Filipino Civilians and the Guerrilla Soldiers and he relayed to me a word-for-word conversation among Roque Tesoro, Jose Tesoro and the Japanese Army Intelligence Officers.

The main objective of the Japanese Army thrusts was the optimum capture of the Guerrilla Leaders; and when the Japanese

Army encountered stiff resistance, the Japanese Army singled me out for capture whether I was dead or alive. Blackhawk was taken into the Japanese Army confidence on the schemes of capturing me, and he took advantage of eliminating other turncoats. The Japanese Army stool pigeons were deputized in locating and reporting my presence to the Japanese Soldiers who swooped down on my lairs. The Japanese Army consuming desire at bagging me ended the lives of many other conspirators. The Japanese Army never suspected that each quisling it loosed on me was virtually at the mercy of the Guerrilla Soldiers the moment the renegades stepped out of the City. The Guides who led them along the routes, were my Guerrilla Soldiers and the betrayers were billeted in the houses of my secret undercover agents until they were let loose on the Guerilla domain, under the watchful eyes of undercover agents. The Fifth Columnists were granted a one-way passage until they met death in unexpected ways; and at least fifty of the traitors perished without setting foot on my hideout in Barrio Bacong.

Blackhawk penetration of the Japanese Army Intelligence Bureau was so subtle that he literally slept at the bedside of the Japanese Chief Kempetai, head of the Japanese Army Intelligence Bureau, and he frequented the Japanese Army War Room. Inside the room of the pre-war government building at Washington Street in Bacolod City, the Japanese Army displayed a huge map of Negros Islands and indicated, with colored pinheads stuck to the map, the plans of attack on targeted places. The arrows revealed the routes the Japanese Army would take and the spots the Japanese Soldiers would assault. The map revealed pronged assaults and the directions from where the attacking Japanese Forces were coming from. The data that Blackhawk supplied me saved my Guerrilla Band and me from complete annihilation by the Japanese Army pincer attacks.

The Japanese Army concentrated their forces and mounted mopping up operations against the Guerrilla Soldiers of Negros Islands; and their armies closed in from the town of San Carlos in the east; Murcia in the north, Barrio Sumag in the west, and

La Carlota in the south. The Japanese Forces planned the encirclement of the Divisional Headquarters and the Free Negros Islands Government sites, and with the aid of collaborators, the Japanese Soldiers found their way to the mountainsides; but the messages of Black hawk which were flashed in advance throughout the Guerrilla Territory, alerted the Guerrilla Soldiers and the Japanese Army punitive expedition ended in dismal failure; even as 500 Japanese Soldiers missed my Guerrilla Soldiers at Sitio Egtalinga, my Rear Command Post, by a mere 100 meters away from their footpaths. The Japanese Soldiers succeeded merely in scuttling the empty stalls of Barrio Bacong market place, but they never captured anybody on their way to their assembly point in the Mambucal Spring Summer Resort. The Guerrilla Soldiers, ordered desistance from attacking the Japanese Soldiers because of superiority of the Japanese Forces, and because of low supply of arms and ammunitions, granted the Japanese Soldiers free passage through the Guerrilla Soldiers territories.

The tightrope, which Blackhawk walked on, stretched to the limit; and the last straw broke when three of my Soldiers were captured by the Japanese Army, and Blackhawk suspected that two of them broke down upon the Japanese Army interrogation, confessed, and made telltale revelations. The culprits were knifed to death, but they had done irreparable damage to our organization; so Black hawk's days were numbered. The end came at a cafeteria in Bacolod City while Policito Salazar was eavesdropping over a cup of coffee, when out of a blue; an acquaintance sidled and whispered to him.

"You are a double agent! You stay here while I fetch the Japanese Soldiers and I will have you arrested!"

The man left for the Japanese Army Contingent while Policito Salazar pondered deeply on the threat that sounded like a thunderbolt to his ears.

How could he determine if the man intended merely on pulling his legs? Fear overcame him and the better part of valor seized him; the time of flight had finally arrived. There was no time left even for bidding his mother good-bye; instead he stocked provisions and spent the rest of the day in hiding, and praying for the merciful night into enveloping the earth and he with darkness, before he could move farther, for the Japanese Soldiers must be on their heels, looking for him.

In the middle of the night, he managed his way out of Bacolod City, filled with apprehensions of capture either by the Japanese Army or by the Guerrilla Soldiers; for like a proverbial bat, the Japanese Army wanted him for desertion, and the Guerrilla Soldiers suspected him of espionage with the Japanese Army. There was no assurance that the Guerilla Soldiers, once he was captured, would honor his only passport to freedom, the password – BLACKHAWK. Disorientation after months inside the Japanese Army zone and the unlighted pathways added to his misery, but he preferred darkness as an ally, to daylight, which was his nemesis. He distanced as far and as fast as he could from Bacolod City, but as dawn approached he found himself far from the safety of the Japanese Army zone. He dreaded any encounter with strangers, but he needed information for the right direction, and he was forced into approaching a cluster of houses where he met an old man from whom he pleaded for information for the right direction, in exchange for some of the provisions he was carrying with him. The old man showed him the way to Mansiliñgan, and he realized that he had wasted valuable time in going round circle at Sitio Bakyas; where he exited to the northeast instead of to the southeast, his destination. He hurriedly headed to Barrio Cansilayan and ultimately crossed Bago River into my Headquarters at Sitio Egtalinga. Policito Salazar explained to me his predicaments even as he relinquished his espionage assignments in Bacolod City. He recommended Felixberto Peña as his successor whom I code-named Specter. Felixberto Peña served the Guerrilla Resistance organization well, but the Japanese Army captured him. He survived captivity and the tortures, but Cesar Medina who was code-named Scorpion replaced him.

In retrospections, Policito Salazar's exploits as a Guerrilla Resistance Movement Counter Spy inside the Japanese Army-held Bacolod City merited an award of commendation. When the Japanese Army lost Jose Tesoro, one of its most productive spies, Blackhawk alerted me of the Japanese Army retaliatory raids into my hideout in Barrio Bacong, and his warnings proved stunningly accurate when the Japanese warplanes bombed and strafed Barrio Bacong at precisely 9 o'clock of a Thursday morning, the time and date which Blackhawk supplied me well in advance of the Japanese Army raids. The areas indicated in the alert notice were all cleared of the Filipino Civilians and the Guerrilla Soldiers while the message was forwarded to the Headquarters of Col. Ernesto Mata. My Soldiers and I distanced from Barrio Bacong and all other Japanese warplane targets; and we stood as spectators to the Japanese warplane bombings and strafing of what proved to be empty targets. Policito Salazar convinced the Japanese Army into sending Gloria Alvaran, a female spy, to captivity of the Guerrilla Soldiers; thus ending her nefarious and deadly spying activities in Negros Islands. Policito Salazar furnished me a photograph of Gloria Alvaran and informed me of the Japanese Army identifying marks on her person. Policito Salazar tipped me off of the Japanese Army Patrols, which initiated our ambush of the Japanese Forces in Sitio Crossing Mining. Blackhawk revealed to me the shipment of weapons from the Bago town Japanese Army Garrison to Bacolod City, which we aborted by killing the Japanese Soldiers in the Garrison before they could effect the shipment, as well as the shipment of kerosene from La Carlota to Bacolod City, which we intercepted at Barrio Sumag. Policito Salazar made possible my active resistance to the Japanese Army, and if we appeared daring in our ambuscades, it was because the advance information imbued as with confidence and assurance of success. Blackhawk tipped us of the Japanese Army movements, which enabled us into setting up well-planned ambuscades, and Blackhawk relayed to us the results of the encounters from the Japanese Army side. It was Black hawk's unequivocal warning message that I passed on to the Divisional Headquarters, of the Japanese Forces desperate battle plan, in exasperation of the Guerrilla Soldiers ambuscades and the threat of the United States Liberation Forces landing in

Negros Islands, of the Japanese Forces marshalling its troops and conducting the "juez de cutsillo," (justice at knife's point); killing on sight anybody the Japanese Soldiers saw and executing to death anyone they caught who stood on their way, during their expeditionary campaign from Barrio Bacong, south, to Barrio Mambucal, north, guided on their way by the Filipinos who were knowledgeable of the mountain terrains and who turned into Japanese Army Spies; yet the Japanese Soldiers failed at catching a single soul because all were forewarned of the approaching dangers from the Japanese Forces.

Policito Salazar asked for assignment outside of Bacolod City, in any capacity he could possibly serve the Resistance Movement; so I endorsed BLACKHAWK to Col. Ernesto Mata for reassignment to the Divisional Headquarters.

CHAPTER 11

Court Martial

Blackhawk's exit from my Outfit portended my personal reverses, as bits of past incidents massed together like the ominous dark clouds before a thunderstorm. Reports of armed men mistreating Filipino Civilians became rampant; as civilians were deprived of their property and members of their family were subjected to abuses. Guerrilla Soldiers fought against each other out of jealousy, rivalry and vengeance when unity was necessary for the defense of the Country. Pillages and lawlessness remained unchecked because civil as well as military laws were put aside and obedience was exacted from the barrel of the guns. Questions were raised which need answers, if the Guerrilla Soldiers succeeded in the elimination of each other, who would be the ultimate beneficiaries of their death? And if chaos and anarchy reigned supreme over the land, to who would the hapless Filipino Civilians turn to for succor? There was a need for discipline and the imposition of law and order for the orderly prosecution of the resistance movement against the Japanese Army, and the regulation governing the conduct of the military personnel in relationship to the Filipino Civilians for their protection and benefit in exchange for their unwavering support and loyalty. Colonel Salvador Abcede who was the most senior officer of the United States Armed Forces in the Far East, in Negros Islands, assumed the position of Negros Islands Commander of the Resis-

tance Movement; in consultation with the Military Governor of
Free Negros Islands, Honorable Alfredo Montelibano, Sr., and
issued a decree for the composition of the Military Court Martial
Tribunal for the prosecution of the bad elements from the Guerrilla Resistance Movement.

I had numerous tiffs with several Guerrilla Leaders, and I stood
accused before the Military Court Martial Tribunal. I had alter-
cations with a Guerrilla Captain which resulted into my stuffing
the barrel of my Pistol into his mouth, and I had disagreements
with a Major over a policy which the Military Governor and the
Deputy Islands Commander approved later, still the rancor of my
disregard of the Major's orders was still palpable.

I looked back to the time when I started my guerrilla activities right after most of the USAFFE Soldiers surrendered to the
Japanese Army, and I was fortunate in the procurement of armaments which was more than any other Guerrilla Leader could
ever dream of possessing, and I was equally lucky in recruiting
men who proved loyal to the Country, until fledgling Guerrilla
movement organizers emerged, who were scouting for weapons
and manpower. The struggle for leadership, weaponry and followers became a squabble among the protagonists for the survival of the fittest in the jungle where danger of ambushes from
fellow Guerrilla Soldiers lurked at every corner of the mountainsides. Since my Guerrilla Outfit had trained Soldiers who were
equipped with weaponry, other Guerrilla Leaders sent feelers
who urged me into joining their ranks; but I refused their overtures because I was uncertain of their motivations, and as a consequence of my adamant refusal, those Guerrilla Leaders sent after me their toughest henchmen with the purpose of taking me
with them at all cost; dead or alive, but I successfully eluded their
entrapments, I recognized the legitimacy of the leaderships of
Honorable Alfredo Montelibano, Sr., as Military Governor of the
Free Negros Islands Government and Colonel Ernesto Mata, as
Deputy Islands Commander of Negros Islands Resistance Movement, who were nearest to my area of operation as a Guerrilla
Unit, in contrast to Col. Abcede who was based farthest in the

southern Negros Islands. I affiliated directly to the two legitimate leaders of the Negros Islands Resistance Movement; and my loyalty to the two gentlemen spawned envy, rancor and animosity from other officers of the top echelon in the Resistance Movement; and the military officers who were closely allied with Col. Salvador Abcede, the Negros Islands Commander, demanded that my head be delivered on a silver platter to the Islands Commander who ordered my court martial trial; as an example of disciplinary action taken and a penalty imposed on an erring Soldier. I knew that the Military Governor and the Deputy Islands Commander would always stand by my side; but there was a need for the restoration of law and order in the military organization, and perhaps there was an opportunity of upholding the orders of the highest officer of Negros Islands Resistance Movement, so the Negros Islands Commander ordered my court martial trial.

I hit the Japanese Soldiers whenever and wherever the vantage points presented and I exploited the advantages to the hilt, although the general policy of the Resistance Movement was a policy of a game of wait and see in conservation of ammunitions; my tactics were misconstrued as intransigence. I executed to death traitors after Intelligence reports confirmed the treachery; but my actuations were misinterpreted as cruelty. I disposed off the inveterate looters, and hanged upside down the thieves until the victims interceded for mercy in their behalf; and I was accused of harshness. I threatened to blow off an Officer's ear, and refused integration into a Captain's group; but the last straw that broke the camel's back was the crime against chastity – rape.

I was summoned to a hearing before the Military High Tribunal and I traveled with 130 of my well-armed Soldiers to Sitio Komalisquis and arrived at the Divisional Headquarters. The Hearing Hall was too small for the accommodation of spectators so my Soldiers stayed at the backyard while they waited for the outcome of court proceedings. Inside the Hearing Hall were the members of the Military Court Martial Tribunal composed of Major Gregorio Café as the Chairman, Roberto Benedicto, Ramon Nolan, Jose Hilado and Luis Baylon as members of the Tribunal.

Lorenzo Teves headed the prosecution panel while the Tribunal appointed Lt. Abao as my Defense Counsel. I dispensed with the services of my Defense Counsel because several things raced into my mind. The proceedings entailed time and tedious efforts in the search and presentation of witnesses for the Accuser and the Accused. As an Accused I would be required the presentation of a Soldier who was responsible for the crime of rape attributed to me. I executed the Soldier to death as a punishment of his crime, so I could no longer produce him in Court; and in fact, the admission that I put him to death would be a crime of murder for which I could be prosecuted criminally for as long as I live. The lengthy trial would also deprive me of battle action in the frontlines, my preoccupation and passion in the first place.

I searched myself for answers to the nagging questions in my mind. What propelled me into organizing a Guerrilla group of Soldiers that fought against the Japanese Army? My mind dwelt on Mereza Tanaka whom I left in Bacolod City and whom I had pledged marriage after the war. Would the results of the Military trial dash my hope into the rocks of disappointment? I mused on the young and beautiful ladies who prepared food, at our prearranged reassembly places after every battle encounter, and who prayed for the success of our ambushes. These young women cared for my Soldiers, and me, and they were mine for the picking as they idolized me because at 25 years old, unmarried, "tall, dark, and handsome" I had scored victories over the Japanese Army. They placed, literally, themselves at my disposal; instead I treated them as my wards, cared for them and looked after their welfare. Did I fight against the Japanese Army for material gain? My answer to the question was illustrated by a rich spinster who offered me nine palm sacks full of Philippine Commonwealth Government bills worth million of pesos which she had saved for years, if only I would defend her sugar cane plantation against the Japanese Army and marauders. I declined her offer because there was no measure of monetary consideration in the performance of my duty inasmuch as I was engaged in a larger task than a protection of one person. I doled out to the neediest whatever

donation she gave me while I pursued a broader mission of fighting against the Japanese Army. Did I resist the Japanese Army in
contemplation of rank advancement? I did not think of military
honors because it was the most chaotic time in the history of the
Philippine Army when the United States Armed Forces in the Far
East disbanded on account of the devastations that the Japanese
Forces dealt on the Philippines. My primary motivation was the
ouster of the Japanese Army from Negros Islands, the objective,
which was threatened by the shifting loyalties of many Filipinos.
One of my Soldiers left my group in disgust because of his displeasure over my battle tactics. Another Soldier departed after I
busted his fingers when I discovered that he stole the property of
other Soldiers, although he stole for me a Japanese Lugger – a
Japanese prized handgun. I dealt punishment to many offenders who were released later; and it was providential that none of
them ever led the Japanese Army into the doorsteps of my lairs
in retaliation for the penalty I imposed on them. I proposed to
fight against the Japanese Army even to death, because I wanted
to teach the Japanese Soldiers an abject lesson that somewhere
in a small patch of earth in Negros Islands, there were Filipinos who knew how to defend their country and freedom. I took
the duty upon myself of defending the helpless Filipino Civilians
against the atrocities of the Japanese Soldiers, because the Government trained me in combat for the defense of my homeland.

As I stood before the Military Court Martial Tribunal, I shud-
dered at the gravity of the punishment for the Articles of War
were explicit on matters of military personnel offenses. The least
of the offenses that I could be tried of was, a conduct unbecoming
of an officer and a gentleman which carried a minimum penalty
of 10 years in prison under hard labor or a maximum of death
penalty with forfeitures of rank and privileges. The prospect of
conviction with capital punishment toyed in my mind an idea
of turning into an outcast. Psychoanalyst believed that inside a
man's personality was an identification mechanism triggered by
dual moral drives constantly in motion; one was good, the other
evil. The drives of hate or evil and love or goodness spring from

man's biological forces of anabolism and catabolism. As I stood before the Military Court Martial Tribunal, my mind swung in a pendulum of indecision. Had the worst of evil forces in me took over control of the situation, I could have ordered my 130-strong and loyal soldiers to load and fire, and killed all the Members of the Court Martial Tribunal and as a consequence, the history of the Philippines would have run a different course because inside that small courtroom were the men who played, in later years, vital roles in the reconstruction of the Republic of the Philippines.

Roberto S. Benedicto became the Philippine Ambassador to Japan, appointed by President Ferdinand E. Marcos; he was instrumental in the Japanese Government reparations of the Philippines. He became an economic and political leader of the Philippines.

Ramon Nolan became a postwar Philippine Ambassador to the United States of America, who was appointed by President Ferdinand E. Marcos. He was a leader in the sugar industry and served his community as a lawyer.

Gregorio Café became a leader of the post war Filipino Veterans organization.

Luis Baylon served in the post war Philippine Army and he became an executive of a reputable commercial bank.

Jose Hilado became a politician and served the Government of Bacolod City, after World War II.

Lorenzo Teves became the Senator of the Philippines, from Negros Oriental, Negros Islands.

These were the men I could have wiped out to death had the evil forces taken held of me; or in desperation my vision blurred by rage and anger, I overlooked the individual identity and military rank of my accusers but saw them all merely as faceless, sitting targets. On the other hand, compassion overtook over my emotions and I pleaded guilty to the charges. I waited for the Tribunal verdict as the Court went into recess for deliberations, so I went back to my Rear Command Post while I resumed fighting against the Japanese Army.

Palpable telltale signs manifested, weeks after the Court Martial Hearing, for I learned with disappointment, that my name was deleted from the roster of officers who were slated for promotion to the military rank of Captain. I had dreamed when I enlisted with the United States Armed Forces in the Far East of becoming a Company Commander, but my aspirations were cut short when World War II erupted and the USAFFE was disbanded until I rose to the rank of First Lieutenant and my aspiration was revived, now that I almost reached my dream, I was denied of the realization of my goal; and shortly thereafter, the Military Court Martial Tribunal handed down its verdict – I was found guilty and I was sentenced to imprisonment. I was reverted back to civilian status, and I was a prisoner. I began to question in my mind the legitimacy of the Court Martial proceedings because of the legal status of the Guerrilla Resistance Movement, which remained unclear. The words of Lt. General Jonathan M. Wainwright of May 7, 1942 over the radio came back ringing in my ears.

"This is Lt. General Jonathan M. Wainwright with a message for General William F Sharp, commanding the Mindanao and Visayan Forces. Anyone receiving this message please notify General Sharp immediately.

"By virtue of the authority vested in me by the President of the United States, I, as Commanding General of the United States Forces in the Philippines, hereby resume direct command of General Sharp and of all troops under his command.

"I will now give another order. Subject: SURRENDER. To put a stop to further useless sacrifice of human lives, I tendered yesterday, May 6 to Lt. Gen. Homma, Commanding General of the Japanese Forces in the Philippines; surrender of the four harbor defense forts. He declined to accept the surrender unless it included the forces under your (General Sharp's) command. I left General Homma without agreement being reached between us. In the name of humanity I decided to surrender the American and Philippine Armies immediately and voluntarily disarm and take the following steps". The Lt. General spelled out the

directions of the surrender of the troops, but he issued the final
warning.

"The Japanese Army and Navy will not cease their operations
unless they fully realize the faithfulness of the execution of these
orders. As they must be carried out faithfully, otherwise the Japanese Forces will not cease their operations."

There was a question of whether the organization of the Negros Islands Resistance Movement was not in contradiction to
the orders of the Commanding General, but as a good Soldier, I
accepted the verdict and I gave up myself to serve the sentences.

The military prison compound was composed of makeshifts
huts clustered on a mountain slope in the Cadiz town area. The
elevation was ringed down to its base with living quarters of soldier inhabitants who made the escape impossible without their
notice. The prison moat was close to another foothill known
among the Guerrilla Soldiers as "Fort Santiago" in reference to
the historical Fort Santiago, which was built during the Spanish
era, in the old walled city of Manila. The Japanese Army imprisoned and tortured Filipinos in the dungeons of the Fort and Fort
Santiago earned a reputation of imprisonment, incarceration,
torture and execution to death.

The prison compound was a dull place except for death executions of prisoners, who were mostly traitors, that broke the
monotony; for when the time came for the execution, I heard
shuffling of heavy feet ascending the top of the hill, then thuds
of picks and shovels against rocky earth pierced the silence, and
the volleys of gun fire punctuated the stillness of the dawn. When
the muted descent of scanty feet scurried back to the compound,
I knew another death sentence was carried out and the funeral
rite was over. Even as one of the prisoners, I had no time for
idleness because the place was crawling with pests that aggravated the punishments. I spent most of my time picking out the
infestisimal plaque of white lice that infested all the seams of my
clothes. The lice sucked human blood and the itchiness caused
sleepless nights that reduced me to a mere bag of bones. My preoccupation was interrupted when Guerrilla Officers arrived in

the Camp and for want of things done; picked on the prisoners to perform errands at their biddings. The prisoners were handy hands for chores as menial as shining boots or as heavy as fetching water and gathering fire woods from distant sources. One of the Officers spotted me and wanted that I dispose of the garbage, which order I refused because I had never relished a household chore in all of my life. The enraged Officer and I almost came into blows until the proverbial cooler heads intervened. The Jail Warden came to my rescue and explained to the Officer the Military Commission orders for all; that any action taken against me should first be referred to the Military Commission. I was the only one who had a status of an untouchable prisoner inside the prison camp.

After four months and twelve days, I was released from imprisonment and the Camp, and I was endorsed to the Divisional Headquarters where I was reassigned to Colonel Ernesto Mata. I was reverted back to military personnel from the status of a civilian, and I was granted a military rank of a Sergeant. Colonel Ernesto Mata, on sending me off to the frontlines, gifted me with the first pistolized Carbine that I had ever seen in the armory of the Philippine Army.

CHAPTER 12

Liberation

I took the pistolized Carbine with a deep sense of gratitude, not knowing that the gun would be an instrument of more deaths from another battle for the recapture of San Carlos from the clutches of the Japanese Imperial Army.

The town of San Carlos marked the boundary between the eastern and western provinces of Negros Islands and provided a gateway to the neighboring island of Cebu, which linked the sea-lanes of the northern to southern Philippines. Nature endowed the town of San Carlos with quays, which berthed the Japanese warships, and the town owned a sugar mill, which supplied sugar and alcohol for war materials. The Japanese Army capitalized on the strategic location of the town and transformed the site into one huge fortification, in its last desperate efforts at staving off the converging American and Filipino Liberations Forces. The concrete buildings of the Mill were altered into embankments, reinforced with thousands of sandbags and pillboxes. Locomotive cars were side-turned for barricades and the iron railroad railings were staked as palisades. The Japanese Imperial Forces honeycombed the town with foxholes, air raid shelters and trenches. Fifteen thousands Japanese Soldiers mounted artilleries, machineguns, and assembled assorted rifles, grenades and other weapons in their arsenal for the defense of the town from the liberating forces, with prospects of more reinforcements and supplies of armaments from the neighboring islands.

In contrast, the United States Liberation Forces landed weapons and ammunitions at the town of Bayawan, 190 kilometers away, southeast, from the embattled town of San Carlos. The Filipino Guerrilla Soldiers moved the war materials to the battle zone with different assaulting battalions staking against the beleaguered town. On November 6, 1944, our battalion established an attacking position at the junction of the Bacolod-Dumaguete national highway and the municipal road leading to the town of San Carlos and participated in the full-scale battle for the recovery of San Carlos from the hands of the Japanese Forces. While the troops to our right under the command of Major Mercado, saturated the areas behind the commercial buildings, the church, and the public market in a thrust towards the San Carlos wharves, the 72nd Engineering Battalion to where I belonged under the command of Major Manuel Jalandoon, concentrated on the well-entrenched Japanese Forces fortifications at the San Carlos Sugar Mills. Behind residential buildings, the drugstores, and the school buildings at one side of the junction roads, our support troops mounted a .45 Caliber Machine guns aimed into the heart of the Japanese Army heavily fortified emplacements. Across the junction roads, platoon of tactical group of soldiers, equipped with grenades and grenade launchers spearheaded a battery of .81 mm cannons.

As a G-2, I was assigned the task of leading the attacking forces and locating the targets, which composed of thousands of Japanese Soldiers rifle slits that were the only avenues into the concreted, thickly walled Japanese Army fortifications. Our tasks involved a three-phase battle operation. The first group to which I belonged, led the formation of the attacking Soldiers and located the tiny portholes of the embankments for the Japanese Soldiers guns, and chipped away the corners of the slits with precision marksmanship until the apertures widened enough for the grenades entrance into the embankments. The grenade throwers took over for the second stage, and fired their grenade launchers enlarging further the holes to accommodate the tips of the cannon balls. The third group composed of Artillery Soldiers, demolished the segmented, concreted fortifications and exposed the Japanese Soldiers to the support group of Filipino Soldiers who assaulted the Japanese Army fortifications with rifle and machine gun bombardments.

As a signal for the commencement of the hostilities, the United States Air Forces strafed the Japanese Forces positions with concentrated firepower of blazing machine guns hoping that the Japanese Forces realized the futility of their resistance and the might of the Liberation Forces; but the Japanese Soldiers stood pat on their grounds. Instead of giving up, the Japanese Forces anti-aircrafts swung into action in retaliation to the incessant United States Air Force bombardments. For several days, the air raids went on toppling water tanks and cutting off food supply but the Japanese Soldiers remained adamantly defiant. They shelled the Liberation Forces with all the armaments in their arsenal in heated exchanges of gun fires and fire powers and the casualties mounted more on the Japanese Army than on the Liberation Forces side since the Liberation Forces were protected by the United States Air Force firepower umbrella; while the Japanese Forces were at disadvantage positions being harassed by the U.S. warplanes and assaulted by the Liberation Forces in a well-planned and well-coordinated attacks against the embattled Japanese Forces. Using another tactical move, the United States Airplanes dropped parachutes which attracted the attention and the curiosity of the Japanese Soldiers who rushed after them and caught the American standards which the Japanese Soldiers grabbed as prized possessions and war treasures, and snatched other chutes that dangled with cartoons of foodstuff; but, thousands of luckless Japanese Soldiers died when they grabbed the lethal bombs that were attached to the parachutes which they mistook for food and souvenirs. A daring United States Airplane Pilot landed his plane on a highway, a few meters from the Japanese Army Defense Line, and the Japanese Soldiers swarmed and encircled the plane into captivity, but the Pilot closed the aircraft canopy, revved his engine and rammed his warplane against the Japanese Soldiers which formed a human barricade; the folded wings of the United States aircraft fooled the Japanese Soldiers into believing that the aircraft was a crippled plane.

The Japanese Soldiers wizened to the American Air Force ploy and concentrated on the battle as it raged on with pitched intensities. Trench mortars zoomed into the Japanese Forces emplacements, blasting away the Japanese Soldiers into smithereens. Machine guns rattled their deadly rain of missiles of leads. Thompson submachine guns sprayed bullets in an unending chain of discharges. Carbines plastered bullets on the Japanese Forces edifices while grenades zeroed into the Japanese Army moats. Grenades after grenades wee lobbed into the Japanese Forces trenches and palisades and the results were utter destructions. The cacophony of gun fires was matched only by the crashing sounds of crumbling structures and the bellowing of smoke from the Japanese Forces defense lines. The intense battle raged for months and the telltale outcome could only be gleaned from the number of rounds of ammunitions expended which averaged 27,000 rounds of ammunitions discharged per minute, day and night, and for months of fighting, and the havoc that the fire power wrought on the Japanese Army defenses; the mangled corpses of the Japanese Soldiers littered the grounds, heap of rubbles and the putrid air pervaded the atmospheres of the battlefields.

There was a threat of the Japanese Forces reinforcements coming from the Islands of Panay and Cebu by sea transport, but the Japanese Forces suffered losses and some of their warships were sank in naval battles. The United States Liberation Forces that landed in Leyte Island on October 20, 1944, paralyzed the Japanese Army and Navy when the Japanese Imperial Forces were caught by surprise by the Liberation Forces landing. The Japanese Forces at San Carlos were left fighting for their lives and they proved of no match to the United States and Filipino Liberation Forces that pounded their battle positions until the Japanese Forces were annihilated.

I learned of a Contingent of Japanese Soldiers in a neighboring islet when the battle subsided, so I departed for the place with eight of my Soldiers from the group that fought with the 72nd Engineering Battalion. We boarded a motorized banca and headed towards the direction, when our banca capsized while we were merely a kilometer away from the shore; and we realized that the banca would no longer float against the waves, when eight soldiers who were fully loaded with arms and ammunitions were on board. We swam desperately back to shore while the sharks tailed after our wakes; and fortunately we reached safely the shore without the necessity of waging a naval battle against the sharks.

The incident of the banca-capsize that soaked me for hours in seawater caused fever in the ensuing days. The chilliness and warmth alternated during the day and nighttime; and the bouts frequented me at regular intervals. Cenon Gatuslao, who was one of my loyal Soldiers and my constant companion, found a safe place for me and entrusted me to the care of the evacuees who were hiding in dwellings built among the tall reeds and grasses out of sight of the town of San Carlos. I requested Cenon Gatuslao to locate our Military Unit and fetch me a Medical Personnel, expecting that Cenon Gatuslao would return within a day or two. My illnesses degenerated while I was waiting for the return of Cenon Gatuslao, and hunger sapped whatever strength was left with me. I was fortunate that Cenon Gatuslao left me with the evacuees who took compassion on me, the family that were composed of aged parents with two daughters. The old couple went on their daily task working on the fields farming for root crops while their two daughters stayed behind and ministered to me. The women scouted for gingers, roasted the root stocks, chopped them to pieces, wrapped the gingers in pieces of cloth and they took turns in rubbing the pack of warm gingers all over my body. I contracted pneumonia that was complicated with malaria and fever never left me alone. The ladies nursed me and showered me with tender care, which was their modest way of expressing gratitude for my efforts in fighting the Japanese Army on their behalf, and their modest contribution to the cause of victory.

A stranger got wind of my presence in the hideout and he knew that I owned a weapon, so he approached me at my sick bed and inveigled me into lending him my firearm on the pretext of hunting game animals for food. I was so sick and tired hearing of his enticements and his annoyance irritated me so much that I told him bluntly I would blast his head off his body if he did not leave the hut after I counted up to 10.

Cenon Gatuslao came back after a couple of weeks with neither a physician nor medicines; and he brought me distressing news that our Troops had departed and had left both of us behind. Cenon Gatuslao devised a crib, loaded me into it, and with the help of volunteers, Cenon and I headed home. We were homeward bound on foot over the rugged mountains of Negros Islands; and the journey over natural barriers along the forest trails was extremely difficult. We were still in the eastern side of the boundary of Negros Oriental (east) and Negros Occidental (west) after three days of travel. My emaciated physical condition deterred me from further journey, so Cenon Gatuslao and I stayed at Barrio Cacao for week's rest before we clambered back to the trails for the next stop. If the trip to Barrio Cacao where we rested for a week was an arduous ascent, the trek to Barrio Gupod, our next destination, was doubly grueling, and the travel in "Gupod" which meant "cutting a plant root down, rock bottom," in Negros Islands Visayan dialect, was a grapple for headway up the mountain walls. It was a place of frantic struggle, taking desperate hold on tree roots in propelling one's self over craggy hills; even then, we still found lighter moments in the midst of our predicaments.

Cenon Gatuslao and I had lumbered, for days, on our way up the mountain trails when an old woman overtook us. The woman, unlike one I knew from the lowlands, walked with complete abandon while she balanced a loaded basket on her head. Cenon Gatuslao and I quickened our steps not believing that an old woman would outdistance us on the same trail; still the old woman kept nonchalantly her steady pace until we finally caught up with her in her house located on the mountaintop. We found also her husband who was lazily strumming on his guitar, and humming lullaby while he stared down the mountain at his wife who was working her way up the rugged trails with heavy load on her head. The Filipinos, by tradition, treated their women with chivalry; and they were expected of carrying the heavy loads in their place, so I wanted to teach the lazy bone a lesson in etiquette but his wife restrained me. I made him cooked a food out of the root crops that his wife brought along with her, as his punishment.

Cenon Gatuslao and I traveled for ten more days before we started our descent into the western side of Negros Islands. The climate of the months of October and November was still a part of the rainy season, which started in July; the trees along the trails oozed with rain water that dampened the grounds we were walking on. We were also soaked wet in our clothes and we parried the incessant attacks from tiny insects that stung us in almost all parts of our body that was left bare. The insects were also formidable adversaries for they zeroed in on our eyes, nose, mouth, and ears and they were always abundant in damp forests. We had more than enough of water supply but food was lacking except when we lodged on houses along the way and the household members were hospitable enough at granting us food and lodging for a night. We found ourselves in most cases, spending nights in caves and subsisting on edible fruits on the waysides. The cold weather and the cold atmospheres of the jungle aggravated the seriousness of my illnesses, but I carried on the trek to as far as my stamina permitted me. It was a roundabout travel without fixed routes and short cuts to a fixed destination; we relied only on hunches and on our scanty knowledge of the terrain in that part of the wilderness of Negros Islands. We stored in our memory the last directional instructions we obtained from the previous and the strangers we met on the way who had lived in some parts of the mountainsides of Negros Islands, and from the sketchy map that they drew for us; we groped our way in the jungle.

Cenon Gatuslao and I arrived in Sitio Komalisquis, the site of the Divisional Headquarters of the North Negros Sector of the Negros Islands Resistance Movement, once a buy hives of resistance against the Japanese Army but now a deserted jungle. The buildings of the Divisional Headquarters were abandoned and the Guerrilla Soldiers gone. I found an individual who stayed behind and I obtained a Skin Bracer compound from him, which I used in rubbing the liquid solution all over my feeble body whenever chills seized me.

We went down to Barrio Bacong and found out that all my Soldiers who were taken over by Lieutenant Tatoy during my absence were gone too. I recalled that my illness started in November of last year when I spent sleepless nights in open air, patiently waiting for the Japanese Army when we laid up ambush entrapments. My lungs weakened and my body natural defenses lessened; and if not for the medical attention of Joaquin Villarosa, a physician, who rendered free medical services to my Guerrilla Soldiers and the medicines which Blackhawk obtained from the drugstores in Bacolod City, I would have died months ago.

The United States Liberation Forces were landing at the wharves of Pulupandan after aerial bombardments that went on even at nighttime, while the Japanese Forces attempted at delaying the Liberation Forces advances by cutting off Bago Bridge, but the advancing American Soldiers shot to death the Japanese Soldier who was tasked at setting off the demolition explosives for the bridge destruction. The Liberation Forces eventually recaptured Bacolod city from the Japanese Army who was fleeing to the northeastern direction.

I found some of my Soldiers when Cenon Gatuslao and I reached Sitio Cabagsiwan, who tipped me off of the presence of the Japanese Soldiers who were hiding behind bushes in Sitio Igcalango. We attacked the Japanese Soldiers lairs and killed them, but we discovered that the group was only a part of the Japanese Army troops hiding nearby. We leveled our weapons, which spewed bullets that wiped out all the Japanese Soldiers. We found map sketches inside the pockets of the dead Japanese Soldiers and we deduced that the troops came from Sitio Crossing Mining, south, but got lost while they were on their way, north, to Barrio Patag, the last Japanese Army stronghold.

CHAPTER 13

Last Stronghold

The reasons remained still unclear why the Japanese Forces chose Barrio Patag as its last bulwark of defense against the American and Filipino Liberation Forces. Patag, as the name implied in Negros Islands Visayan dialect meant "plateau," a patch of earth hewn from the mountain walls of Marapara Mountains, 20 kilometers east of Silay, and a town 15 kilometers north of Bacolod City. Barrio Patag was accessible, although barred by dozens of mini hill, through a few kilometers of oblique hike northeast of Bacolod City, ascending to the dense forest of the Marapara Mountains.

The desperate Japanese Forces dashed stealthily to the sanctuaries of Barrio Patag while the United States Liberation Forces made beachhead landings at Pulupandan, 43 kilometers south of Bacolod City, obviously avoiding casualties of the Filipino Civilians while the Liberation Forces closed in a recapture of Bacolod City from the control of the Japanese Army. It was not an easy retreat because the Japanese Forces sensed the impending doom from all flanks as the United States and the Filipino Guerrilla Liberation Forces cut off the Japanese Forces military links from San Carlos, the potential reinforcement sources of the Japanese Forces from the neighboring islands to the Japanese Army in Bacolod City.

Months before the United States Liberation Forces landed in Negros Islands, there were clear signs of deliverance from the control of the Japanese Forces when the United States Air Force delivered selective bombings of Japanese Army defense installations but the stubborn Japanese Soldiers laughed off the aerial bombardments to the quizzical Filipino Civilians, as "American bluffs"; and the Japanese Soldiers boasted that whatever the United States Air Forces destroyed the Japanese Soldiers repaired. The Japanese Soldiers struggled doggedly in restoring the Bacolod City airport, which the Japanese Air Forces utilized for the operations of their warplanes. The Filipino Civilians, whom the Japanese Army hired as laborers, filled the craters caused by the United States Air Forces strikes; the Japanese Air Forces hid their planes under coconut palm trees but the continuing air strikes dissipated whatever efforts the Japanese Army exerted in the reconstruction of the devastations. The Japanese Army problems were complicated by the United States Air Forces incursions over the skies of Negros Islands, when the American Fighter planes engaged the Japanese Zero airplanes in dogfights. The United States Air Force Lightning planes materialized from the clouds, in unexpected moments, and chased the Japanese Zero fighter planes; the aerial battles were oftentimes fought at low altitudes that the maneuvers brought the opposing pilots so close that they stared from eyeballs to eyeballs with each other. The aerial battles reduced the number of the Japanese Zero fighter planes until finally only a solitary Japanese plane was seen, just before dusk, hugging treetops in a surreptitious reconnaissance of the desolate horizon; and then the Japanese warplane disappeared completely from the skies of Negros Islands.

The Japanese Forces on the ground fared less because defeat threatened them. The United States Air Forces signaled the liberation of the town from the Japanese Army when American planes dropped, in a lazy afternoon, a couple of bombs at the outskirt of Murcia. There was a pause in the aerial bombardment, but the United States warplanes came back in the succeeding days and strafed, the town municipal building, with machine gun fires. The assaults were precise and systematic as U.S. planes flew from the south to the north, and plastered the municipal building with bullets as the planes turned back for another rounds of aerial attacks against the Japanese Army inside the Garrison. The Japanese Soldiers had barricaded themselves inside the municipal building by the time the Filipino Civilians had evacuated the town, the United States Airplanes had strafed the building, and the Guerrilla Soldiers had ringed the town while they assaulted the Japanese Soldiers inside the Garrison. The Guerrilla Soldiers established a kilometer perimeter attacking line around the Japanese Army Garrison and assaulted the municipal building with the entire war arsenal in their possession; the assault was a display of firepower, which the Guerrilla Soldiers received as war material supplies from the United States Liberation Forces. The Guerrilla Soldiers attacked using Carbines, Thompson Submachine guns, Garands, Rifle Grenades, bazookas, and trench mortars with thousands of rounds of ammunitions. The Japanese Soldiers abandoned the use of their observation tower, stayed inside the building, and fortunately for the Japanese Soldiers, the town municipal building was constructed of solid concrete masonry; that only one mortar shell penetrated the wall of the structure. The Murcia town municipal building which the Japanese Soldiers occupied as Garrison was pock-marked with all kinds of bullets from the United States Airplane machine gun strafing and Guerrilla Soldiers ground assault, but the Japanese Soldiers never fought back. The Guerrilla Soldiers, after weeks of assault and for unknown reason, ceased the attack and left the town. The Japanese Soldiers who survived the assault moved to the Catholic Church building, twenty feet away, burned their dead companions, crossed the national highway, and crawled towards the Langub Creek. The much-feared Japanese Soldiers, from this point on, existed as fugitives and survived on a day-to-day basis while they groped, on foot, their way north to Patag. The fate of the Japanese Soldiers from the town Garrison of Murcia was similar to all other Japanese Soldiers who manned the Japanese Army Garrisons until the United States Liberation

Forces scuttled them before they could assemble for an orderly retreat to the Japanese Forces last stronghold in Barrio Patag. The Japanese Soldiers slept inside culverts during daytime and snaked their way to the northeasterly direction during the night. They fed on corns when they came upon cornfields, sugar canes, and they stole food from houses they passed by on the way.

A farmer was very surprised at the disappearance of his food, which he locked inside a cabinet in his kitchen while he replenished continuously his food supply as soon as they were gone. The farmer in exasperation, devised a trap for the felon, and to his astonishment, he bagged a Japanese Soldier. The Japanese Soldiers went hungry, tired and exhausted; they slept under bridges, inside caves, water canals, and ditches with mere grasses as canopies. Thousands died of starvation, exhaustion, and capture by the Filipino Civilians who hacked them to death with bolos. A few of the Japanese Soldiers resisted capture and killed their pursuers for it appeared that a Japanese Soldier had always a last bullet reserved for his Captor. The rest of the Japanese Soldiers who survived the snail's-pace advance reached Patag where the Japanese Forces established the last stand against the Liberation Forces.

Murcia was festive in celebration of the liberation from the Japanese Army, when I reached the town. There was not much for me to do but go to Bacolod City; so I hitchhiked on an army truck for a ride to Bacolod. Strangers, whom I encountered in Bacolod City, gawked at me because I was emaciated, I wore ragged clothes, belts of ammunitions and I carried guns; and to them I must have appeared like a hobo and a soldier at the same time. A friend, however, who saw me shrunken, fed me to my heart's content, then I searched for the Military Authorities and I presented myself to the Military Camp where I was processed and I was assigned to 74th Philippine Regimental Combat Team. Our Regiment moved to Barrio Patag for the final battle against the Japanese Forces that fortified the mountainside of Marapara Mountains.

The United States Liberation Forces landing in Pulupandan, 43 kilometers south of Bacolod City provided the Japanese Army time for retreat. The Guerrilla Soldiers left the mountains and headed towards the seacoast at the same time that the United States Liberation Forces were landing for the assault towards Bacolod City, against the Japanese Army main forces, and left a vacuum in the mountains to which the retreating Japanese Forces filled at Barrio Patag. The United States Liberation Forces and the Guerrilla Soldiers pursued the retreating Japanese Forces, which fortified Barrio Patag so strongly, that the joint American and Filipino Liberation Forces encountered extremely stiff resistance from the Japanese Forces.

The thick forest trees concealed the Japanese Forces while the walls of Marapara Mountains offered formidable barriers against the pursuing American and Filipino Liberation Troops. The Japanese Soldiers were in suicidal mood and they were never in a position of granting an inch of their ground defenses to the Liberation Forces. The Japanese Army tied as many Snipers to as many treetops in the forest trees and shot to death every single Liberation Soldier who appeared on the Sniper's cross-hair gun sight. It took several days of fighting and sustaining heavy casualties before the United States Army discovered the Japanese Army tricks, and the United States Soldiers retaliated with deadly accuracy; they felled with bullets the Japanese Army Snipers from the treetops. The United States Liberation warships that were anchored at the Bacolod City seafronts shelled the Japanese Forces defensive positions in Barrio Patag, and the naval bombardments hit accurately their targets as chunks of earth were blasted away from the mountain walls hideout of the Japanese Forces, still the Japanese Army stood their grounds. The United States Liberation Forces air strikes pounded heavily on the mountain fortifications of the Japanese Forces but the Japanese Forces were deeply imbedded under the canopy of thick forests, so the United States ground troops utilized flame throwers in defoliating and scorching the forest and the mountain wall stronghold of the Japanese Army.

The 74th Philippine Regimental Combat Team fought side by side with an American Regiment against the Japanese Forces that were well entrenched in the mountainside of Marapara Mountains, and for several weeks the battle was fought fiercely by both the Liberation Forces and the Japanese Forces.

We, Soldiers of the 74th Philippine Regimental Combat Team, were placed between the American Regiment and the Japanese Forces defense line, when a Squad of Japanese Soldiers sneaked past our attacking position, towards the American Regiment Artillery group and knocked out the United States Artillery before half of the Japanese Squad of Soldiers perished and the other half was captured. The United States Army Officers elicited information from the Captives that the Japanese Soldiers would rather die than surrender to the Filipino Soldiers. The United States Liberation Forces pulled out, on the following morning, the 74th Philippine Regimental Combat Team from the battlefields of the American Liberation Forces and the Japanese Army stronghold in Patag, and our Regiment was sent back to Bacolod City.

The battle for the Japanese Army stronghold in Patag raged for months and the United States Liberation Forces were at a loss as to the actual number of the Japanese Soldiers holding out in the rugged terrains of the Marapara Mountains. The naval shelling from the coast, which was guided by the U.S. reconnaissance planes inflicted devastations on the hillside while the U.S. Aircraft Bombers delivered more bombs and machine gun fire power that complemented the ground assault of the United States Army Troops. The difficulty of dislodging the Japanese Soldiers from the forests of Patag could be gleaned from the situation where the United States 503rd Paratroopers fought side by side with the United States Infantry rather than dropped from the air and fought their way into the Japanese Army stronghold, because of the density of the forest trees that screened the Japanese Army defenses from the skies. The Japanese Army scattered their Soldiers to as many hills nearby and they fortified the top vantage points while the United States and the Philippine Liberation Forces were attacking from the base of the hills. Knob Hill was one of the Japanese Army fortifications that stood between Patag and other hills down to the Marapara Mountains southern range. The battle for the recapture of Knob Hill from the Japanese Army was so intense and difficult that the battle alarmed no less than General Doughlas Mac' Arthur. It was to the credit of the Filipino Guerrilla Soldiers who were reorganized into Philippine Regimental Combat Teams, which guided and fought alongside the United States Liberation Forces that dealt the Japanese Forces the final blow. The Japanese Soldiers, instead of surrendering, moved south of the Marapara Mountains. The United States Army, sensing that the Japanese Soldiers would never surrender to the Filipino Guerrillas secured the frontlines from Patag to Santa Rosa, a Barrio down the southernmost plateau of Marapara Mountains, where thousands of bearded, long-haired, haggard and impoverished Japanese Soldiers gave up the struggle. Of the estimated 31,000 Japanese Soldiers who held the Liberation Forces at bay in Patag, only an estimated of 14,000 Japanese Soldiers survived the battle and surrendered to the United States Army. The United States Army Soldiers loaded the Japanese Army Soldiers into the United States Duck Cars and transported them from Santa Rosa to Bacolod City where people and even school children along the highway pelted the hapless Japanese Soldiers with stone pebbles until the United States Soldiers who escorted the Convoys fired warning shots into the air scaring away the Filipino Civilians. The Municipality of Murcia was finally ridden of the Japanese Army.

I was integrated with the United States 53rd Regimental Infantry Division, right after my Regimental Combat Team was pulled out from Patag, and I was sent to Sibulan, Negros Oriental where I underwent rigid military training such as; running in broad jump between emptied 20-gallon barrels that were set 10 feet apart with my body loaded with 25-pound of weapons and military supplies. The idea was clearing the distances between the barrels while I balanced my weight on movable barrels without breaking the tempo, and climbing over the walls at the end of the maneuver; and walking under water with the same weight using pipes for breathing while submerged in the river. The military training was rigid and more comprehensive because we were on an important mission; we were to land and assault the Japanese Forces at Iwo Jima, Japan. We were near the disembarkation point from the United States Sea Transports when our Officers received the message that Japan had surrendered and we turned back for Negros Islands because World War II had finally ended.

CHAPTER 14

Japanese Matrimony

The nightmares of World War II receded in my memory but the portrait of Mereza Tanaka lingered vividly in some corner of my mind. Hakaro Tanaka, Mereza Tanaka's father died years before the Japanese Army invaded Negros Islands, nevertheless, the Japanese Army adopted Mereza Tanaka and her family as among the Japanese Civilian wards; yet the integration of the Tanaka family into the conduit of the Japanese Army was never without an acid test of her loyalty to the Japanese Crown.

When Mereza and I parted ways at the inception of World War II, I never had an illusion that we would meet again, while Mereza harbored an eerie feeling of my survival. Many of the Filipinos who switched allegiances as Japanese Army Spies were my contemporaries who ripped wide open my romantic link to her; and the Japanese Army Intelligence Bureau discovered her special relationship with me, a Soldier of the United States Armed Forces in the Far East (USAFFE), so Mereza was considered a Japanese Army security risk. The Japanese Army interrogated her methodically, dangling carrot of Japanese Army protection as a reward for her loyalty and hanging a stick of death over her head at the slightest sign of treachery. Mereza Tanaka parried adeptly the Japanese Army inquisitions by admitting her relationship with me, that was nurtured before World War II began, but she maintained that the romantic link between us was completely severed after hostilities broke out between the USAFFE Soldiers and the Japanese Army.

The Japanese Intelligence Bureau shadowed her every move and placed her under watchful eye round the clock, which accounted for the reason why our only tryst in her house at Gonzaga Street during my reentry of Bacolod City, never materialized. The Japanese Army Spies, who nurtured secret love for her, exploited to the hilt our tie-up by threatening its exposure to the Japanese Army with an aim of softening her heart into accepting their love overtures. The Japanese Army Spies supplied the Japanese Army Secret Agents with dossiers against Mereza Tanaka, which unfailingly evinced the Japanese Army intense grilling of her with dire threats to her life. The Japanese Army Informers trifled with Mereza Tanaka's sensibilities while supplying the Japanese Army with false information in their attempt at breaking down her heart. The Japanese Army Spies spread spurious news of my capture and death indicating to Mereza my whereabouts, and inquired if Mereza would view my body before I was buried. The Japanese Army Spies fished for her slightest reaction, which would betray her thoughts and incriminate herself. Mereza held back her instincts and curiosity and maintained her stoic composure while she controlled her gnawing solicitude deep inside her heart, for my welfare. She volunteered working in the Japanese Army hospitals ministering to the wounded Japanese Soldiers in attestation to her loyalty to the Japanese Army. My Japanese Army Counter Spy was also busy hovering over her at the background, as I had given orders for her protection against imminent danger from the Japanese Soldiers, Japanese Army Spies, and even from other Guerrilla Soldiers.

The Japanese Army took along with them all the Japanese Civilians when they fled to the mountains in Patag; the Japanese non-combatants composed of Japanese Nationals who resided in Negros Islands for several years before World War II, and were mostly aged men and women, teenagers and children. The Japanese Nationals were organized into Japanese Civilian Associations with membership numbering 2,000 Japanese civilians from all over Negros Islands. The Japanese Army constructed hastily a warehouse at Patag *Daku* (bigger plateau) where the belongings of the Japanese Civilians were shipped in advance of the arrival of the Japanese Civilians; but the United States Liberation Forces bombed the warehouse setting the depot and all its contents to flames.

The Japanese Army transported the Japanese Civilians to Sitio Guimbalaon, the last stop for the Japanese Army vehicles and the first step of a trek on foot to the mountain hideouts. The ascent was extremely difficult for the senior Japanese Citizens who traipsed on footpaths, which hardly accommodated traffic at a time. The youngsters persuaded the hesitant, wheedled them, and hauled them in a frantic, snail's paced climb to the sanctuary of the jungle. Mereza and other teenaged girls were assigned at transporting and assisting the infirmed old men and women in the journey into the dense forests; the girls took turns in holding the feeble hands, pushing the hesitant bodies, and towing the aged and weak men and women, one at a time on the precipices, beside cliffs, and into the secluded caves. The unpredictable respites from the Liberation Forces bombardments dictated the tempo of decampment as the Escapees winded slowly their way under forest growths and evaded luckily the hail of bullets that whizzed past their locations.

The Japanese Army divided the Japanese Civilians into smaller units and settled them in caves in the jungle; while the Japanese Soldiers consolidated their forces in desperate attempts at staving off the tide of battle against the advancing Liberation Forces. Truckloads of American Soldiers died in the final drive against the Japanese Forces in the battle of Patag, while a number of Filipino Guerrilla Soldiers lost their lives. Both sides of the fighting Forces waged ferocious battle against each other which prompted the American Forces the deployment of the warships bombardments and the naval artillery shelling, the ground troop assaults and the air strikes that concentrated on the fastnesses of Sitio Guimbalaon, Patag, and the Marapara Mountains and dealt the Japanese Forces the lethal and conclusive blows.

When the rain fell on the month of July 1945, the caves where the Japanese Soldiers and the Japanese Civilians hid dripped like leaking roofs and the damp earth exacerbated the miseries of the Japanese Soldiers and the Japanese Civilians. The lack of food forced the non-combatant Japanese Civilians into scavenging edible roots of forest growths, but the lack of nutriments wasted away the starved bodies of both the Japanese Soldiers and the Japanese Civilians. Mereza's ministration to the wounded Japanese Soldiers proved futile and hopeless in the absence of drugs and nourishments; especially when more wounded Japanese Soldiers piled up daily on temporary bamboo beds, than those who were restored to health or died.

The Japanese Army Officers saw enough sufferings and realized the hopelessness of the military positions, so the Japanese Army Officers gathered the Japanese Civilian Leaders for final instructions; each Leader would lead his group to the nearest American Liberation Forces camp for surrender. The Tanaka, Togue, Machumoto, and Marunaga family members chose the northern route of exit, and wandered into Victorias, a town twenty kilometers north of Patag. The Japanese Civilian Group first contact with the Filipinos proved to be a scary encounter because the Filipino Band was a militia force of the Filipino Guerrilla Soldiers, and the para-military men wanted the massacre of the Japanese Civilian Group, the eldest Marunaga family member and the Leader of the Group was chosen first to die. It was providential that the para-military Soldiers learned, somehow, that the Machumoto family members hailed from Cadiz, a neighboring town where some of the Militia Soldiers resided; the Japanese Civilian Group earned the sympathy of the Filipino Militia Force which spared all the member of the Japanese Civilian Group from death. The Filipino Militia Force conducted, after monetary inducements were paid, the Japanese Civilian Group to the nearest lodging houses which the para-military Filipino Forces guarded during the night, and who procured a truck for transportation, the following day, and who transported the Japanese Civilian Evacuees to the nearest American Army Detachment where the Japanese Civilians surrendered.

I searched for Mereza Tanaka, immediately after World War II ended, among the Japanese Prisoners of war who were incarcerated inside the Provincial Jail in Bacolod City. As a Soldier of the victorious Liberation Forces, I had privileges of attesting to the loyalty of Japanese Civilians to the cause of the Guerrilla Resistance Movement. As a Leader of Guerrilla Soldiers, the Military Tribunal Commission that tried Collaborators to the Japanese Army in Negros Island called me; many were convicted while others were acquitted on my testimonies. I utilized the privilege in vouching for the innocence of Mereza Tanaka, and I secured her release from the United States Army prison camp. The Japanese Civilians who surrendered to the United States Liberation Forces were incarcerated in the Provincial Jail in Bacolod City. Most of the Japanese Civilians opted for the movement of Japanese Army from Barrio Patag down the Marapara Mountain ranges and they ended up in Sta. Rosa, a Barrio of Murcia, at the southernmost part of the Marapara Mountains. The Japanese Civilians were as bedraggled, and as famished as the Japanese Soldiers. They were part of the Japanese Soldiers that composed an estimated 14,000 Japanese Soldiers who surrendered to the United States Liberation Forces at Barrio Sta. Rosa, Municipality of Murcia, and Province of Negros Occidental in Negros Islands, Philippines that ended World War II in Negros Islands. The Japanese Civilians sobbed, wept, wailed, and cried when they learned that I, a Guerrilla Soldier bailed out Mereza Tanaka, daughter of Hakaro Tanaka, a Japanese Citizen for they never suspected a romantic link between us; and the they felt that Mereza Tanaka, a fellow Japanese betrayed her friends, countrymen and the Japanese Army. The truth of the matter was that Mereza Tanaka had never supplied me with any military information against the Japanese Army, for I had a very able Japanese Army Counter Spy in the person of Black hawk.

EPILOGUE

Master Sergeant Jorge G. Herrera, Jr., after World War II served as Malacañang Guard and he was detailed as body guard and driver of Honorable Alfredo Montelibano, Sr., who was the Secretary of National Defense and at the same time Secretary of Interior under the administration of President Sergio Osmeña, Sr. It was during these assignments that Jorge G. Herrera, Jr. foiled assassination attempts on the lives of high Government Officials in Malacañang Palace when he uncovered explosives hidden among fruits inside the baskets that were camouflaged as gifts to the Government Officials. With combat experience, he was assigned as Platoon Leader and fought against the HUKBALA-HAP, a dissident movement in the mountains of Luzon Island.

The Hukbong Bayan Laban Sa Hapon (HUKBALAHAP) had its base of operation in its sanctuary, in the wilderness of the Cordillera Mountains of northern Luzon Island, but it extended its militant influence among the rice farmers of the Central Plains of Luzon for two reasons; the assurance of food supply from the products of the farmers, and the enlistments of the disgruntled tenant framers into the ranks of the rebel movement. The HUKBALAHAP or HUKs for short, mounted guerrilla warfare against the Armed Forces of the Philippines and staged hide-and-seek ambushes. The HUKs mingled with the peasants at daytime, but they roamed, fully armed, during the night hunting for the Philippine Army Soldiers. Lieutenant Herrera's platoon unit decamped during a night among the stacks of rice straws that were scattered on the rice fields in the Candaba Swamps of Central Plains of Luzon which was notably the hotbeds of the HUKBALAHAP; each Soldier hid in a haystack of rice straws while the Philippine Soldiers stayed alert for possible HUKs attack, when Lieutenant Herrera intercepted a walkie-talkie call from his Platoon Sergeant asking for his specific location. Lt. Jorge G. Herrera, Jr. supplied his Platoon Sergeant with false positions, and to his astonishment, each sham position he pinpointed to was shelled with precision by the HUK's mortar fires. He realized finally that his life was in danger, and he obtained an answer to why so many courageous and valuable Platoon Leaders were slain and their lives wasted in the battlefields of the Central Plains of Luzon. He concluded that the HUKBALAHAP had infiltrated the ranks of the Armed Forces of the Philippines. He dreaded the thought of killing his Countrymen; fortunately, he was reassigned to the Philippine Armed Forces Motor Pool in the capital City of Manila and avoided similar fates that befell the dedicated and valiant Platoon Leaders before him.

Jorge C. Herrera, Jr. served the Armed Forces of the Philippines in Luzon Island, but he wanted a reunion with his family who resided in Negros Islands, so he requested for a transfer of assignment to Negros Occidental; unfortunately, such request for transfer was a violation of the Military protocol, and in fact Herrera, for requesting such a transfer, was subject to Court Martial proceedings. Secretary of National Defense and Interior, Honorable Alfredo Montelibano, Sr. came to his rescue. Secretary Montelibano gave General Calixto Duque of the Armed Forces of the Philippines a choice: approval of Herrera's request or resignation as Chief of Staff of the Armed Forces of the Philippines. General Duque approved Herrera's request for transfer of assignment on a condition that Herrera's military rank be reduced from Lieutenant to Master Sergeant. Master Sergeant Jorge G. Herrera, Jr. served further in the Armed Forces of the Philippines until his retirement on military compulsory age and he was discharged honorably from the roster of the Armed Forces of the Philippines. It was Honorable Alfredo Montelibano, again, who was the Economic Adviser to the Philippine President Ramon Magsaysay, who recommended Jorge G. Herrera for employment with the National Rehabilitation and Reforestation Administration (NARRA) in Bacolod City where he retired from government service at the compulsory age of 65 years.

As a Civilian, a powerful Politician from northern Negros Islands, approached him for the assassination of a political rival with an offer of half a million pesos, but Jorge G. Herrera, Jr. laughed off the offer, saying that he killed only for a conviction. He pulled a trigger when provoked up to a point when a human being appeared blurry in his vision, and a person became unrecognizable and a faceless target. It was at this point when he disregarded military rank, and the social status of his target, much less the consequences of his action. Jorge G. Herrera, Jr. lived his life as a civilian in stark contrast to his life in the military organization when he initiated battles against the Japanese Army whenever and wherever the advantages presented in his favor.

Members of the New People's Army (NPA), successor to the HUKs approached him into joining the rebel ranks, but Jorge G. Herrera, Jr. advised them into giving up to the Philippine Government, admonishing them that the Philippine Government had a long arm, and sooner or later the Philippine Government would catch up with the Rebels.

Master Sergeant Jorge G. Herrera, Jr. remained loyal to the Philippine Government until his death. M/Sgt. Jorge G. Herrera, Jr., a Soldier, who dared the Japanese Army, fought them against overwhelming odds and lived to tell his story; died on August 4, 1992. He died a poor man and he was interred in a cheap grave that was placed on top of his uncle's (Teodorico Garagara) tomb, in accordance with his death wish, and was buried in the municipal cemetery of the town of Murcia, Province of Negros Occidental in Negros Islands, Philippines.

§§§

Printed in the United States
By Bookmasters